THE CHANGING FACE of the CHURCH

THE
CHANGING
FACE of the
CHURCH

FROM AMERICAN TO GLOBAL

Thomas G. Nees

Beacon Hill Press of Kansas City
Kansas City, Missouri

Copyright 1997
by Beacon Hill Press of Kansas City

ISBN 083-411-6723

Printed in the
United States of America

Library of Congress Cataloging-in-Publication Data
Nees, Thomas G., 1937-
     The changing face of the church : From American to global / Thomas G. Nees.
     p.   cm.
     Includes bibliographical references.
     ISBN 0-8341-1672-3 (pbk.)
     1. Church of the Nazarene—Membership.   2. Holiness churches—United States—Membership.   3. United States—Religion—20th century.   4. Christianity—20th century.   5. Christianity—Forecasting.   I. Title.
BX8699.N35N45   1997
287.9'9—dc21   97-11266
                                                                                                     CIP

10   9   8   7   6   5   4   3   2   1

Contents

Acknowledgments

I wish to express my appreciation to those who have contributed to this book in special ways.

First, my gratitude to General Superintendent John A. Knight and Church Growth Director Bill M. Sullivan for their encouragement to build an open, inclusive church. They have set the pace and opened the door for all Nazarenes to expand the boundaries of our church.

A word of thanks is in order to those whose names appear with their quoted remarks. Each of them took time from busy schedules for an interview, offering insight for the future of the church they serve and love. Their ideas make this a book of wisdom as well as information. One of the most enjoyable tasks of this writing project was listening to them and learning from them. Thanks to José Pacheco, Charles Johnson, Paul Orjala, Jean Cidel, Roger Bowman, Russ Bredholt, Jerry Porter, Jack Stone, Robert Scott, Nina Gunter, Ken Crow, Jesse Middendorf, Ray Hurn, Dale Jones, Dallas Mucci, and Johnny Nells.

To the members of the Multicultural Ministries strategy committees, people of different languages and cultures who have invited me to worship and break bread together, I owe a special debt. They are bringing to the church rich traditions, helping us better understand the gospel and one another.

For the encouragement to finish the manuscript in a short time I want to thank the editors at Nazarene Publishing House.

And to my wife, Pat, I am most indebted. She has read and reread the manuscript, correcting and editing. But much more—her partnership in ministry through the years, her strong love of people from every culture, especially the downtrodden, has kept me aware of the beauty in all God's children.

Introduction

In my former Silver Spring, Maryland, neighborhood near Washington, D.C., I would often visit the local bank. It was not uncommon to stand in line, look around, and realize that I was the only English-speaking white customer waiting to make a deposit or cash a check. The young tellers were all bilingual minorities, recruited and trained to serve our increasingly diverse neighborhood. In the few—or not so few—minutes standing in those lines, I would look at the people and wonder: Where had they come from? What must it be like to move to the United States? How were they getting along in this neighborhood? Most of them were in working clothes—construction workers, grocery clerks, fast-food workers. I wondered how they were making it financially. I didn't know their languages, and they couldn't speak English well enough to hold a conversation. We smiled a lot.

In the supermarket across the street from the bank, the shelves were beginning to display foods I didn't recognize. New stores with international themes were opening in the nearby shopping centers. Our schools and churches, as well as our restaurants and shopping centers, were full of people coming to America primarily from the Asian and Hispanic worlds.

The beginning of this wave of new immigrants to the United States and Canada began to be noticeable following the Vietnam War. Earlier in the 20th century, immigrants seeking asylum from war-torn Europe came to America in great numbers, but they didn't change the landscape that much. Although many of the earlier immigrants didn't speak English, they looked pretty much like the rest of us, and so they fit in or assimilated very quickly. But not so with the new immigrants.

Following the Vietnam War, our family agreed to sponsor a refugee family from South Vietnam. I remember well the day in 1975 when my wife and I took our four children, ages 6 to 13, to Washington National Airport to welcome our new friends, a Vietnamese family—father and mother and their six children, ages 2 to 14—who had been flown to us from their temporary shelter at an Arkansas military base. In the rush of resettlement following the war, there was not much paperwork and no preparation. We had no idea what to expect. We just agreed that we wanted to help a homeless refugee family and would make the adjustments necessary to live together in the rather large parsonage provided us by Washington First Church of the Nazarene.

The father was a former officer in the South Vietnamese navy. He spoke enough broken English to translate for all of us. For our family it was an exciting, expanding experience that ended all too soon when we were able to help them find work and a decent, even if humble, place to live. As we look back, we realize that we didn't have to go to Vietnam to learn about the war or Southeast Asia. Through their experiences we learned about a country we have yet to visit. We learned to appreciate their traditions, their values, their loyalty to family, and even their Christian faith as practiced quite differently from our own.

And we became their gateway to America. We introduced them to our neighbors, enrolled the children in schools, led them through the supermarkets and shopping malls, assisted them in applying for jobs and housing, and invited them to church. In all these experiences and more, both families were changed. We didn't think much about it then, but our families were a microcosm of the changes that were taking place in many homes, neighborhoods, and churches, and would soon affect everyone.

In just a few years now we'll enter a new century, a new millennium, and if some predictions and forecasts are correct, a new age. The United States and Canada, the home base of the Church of the Nazarene since its beginning nearly 100 years ago, is undergoing profound population shifts that will forever change the way we view the world and ourselves.

In the fall of 1993 *Time* magazine published a special issue on "The New Face of America: How Immigrants Are Shaping the World's First Multicultural Society." The cover picture was a composite of a beautiful young woman with features blending the several various racial groups that make up American society. In the articles, *Time* cited demographic statistics that have become common knowledge by now. In the greatest wave of immigration since 1901-10, 1 million immigrants enter the United States annually, most of them from the Asian and Hispanic worlds. Sometime in the mid-21st century, minority groups will make up the majority. The English-speaking white population will itself become the largest minority group, comprising less than 50 percent of the total population.

While the Church of the Nazarene does not yet "look like" America and Canada, the face of the church is also changing.[1] These demographic changes present the church with both challenges and opportunities. The "new face of America" and the changing world order will dramatically alter the way the church pursues its mission. Until very recently, the Nazarene world has been divided between the "sending" church and the "receiving" church. The church in the United States and Canada (with a few exceptions) was a sending or missionary church. The rapid growth of the Church of the Nazarene in 20th-century America was in the context of what most people understood to be a Christian nation in what some thought to be the "Christian century."[2] American Christians did evangelism at home and missions abroad. While there was such a thing as "home missions" for a while, it was always assumed even until the present that real missionary work goes on for the most part in the non-English-speaking, non-Christian countries of the world. The stereotypical missionary is an American who crosses an ocean or border, learns another language, adapts to a foreign culture, introduces the gospel, and plants the church eventually to be led by the indigenous population.

All this is changing. America is becoming as secular as it is diverse and is about to be declared a mission field in its own right. A decade ago Jerry Appleby anticipated much of this in his book *Missions Have Come Home to America: The Church's Cross-cultural Ministry to Ethnics.*[3] When *Time* claimed in its title that America is "the world's first multicultural society," it didn't ignore other countries with minority populations and cultural diversity. It is simply that something unique is happening here and now. People are coming to the United States and Canada from all over the world. While a few of the new immigrants are refugees seeking asylum, most come voluntarily (occasionally illegally), looking for their place and opportunity in a society that is beginning to look like the world. Some come at great personal risk and expense. In every instance they are willing to uproot themselves, leaving family and friends, to seek a new life in what has again become the "New World."

For the Church of the Nazarene there is one significant difference that sets us apart from secular society. While immigrants are new to the United States and Canada, many of these immigrants are Nazarenes. The face of the church in the United States and Canada is being changed by the presence of immigrant Nazarenes of different cultures and languages coming to us as products of our own missionary work abroad. This new wave of immigrants has swept in thousands of Nazarenes, including trained leaders, pastors, and even district superintendents, looking for their place in the American and Canadian church.

In this book I've distinguished immigrant minorities from historic minorities. Historic minorities include Native Americans, African-Americans, and Mexican Americans. Native Americans and other indigenous people were present before their land was occupied by Old World explorers and settlers. African-Americans were, of course, involuntary immigrants and have been present in American society from the earliest colonial days. The church is underrepresented in all these historic minority groups. It may be that these immigrant Nazarenes will become bridge people, helping, perhaps forcing, the church to become more inclusive.

In the early 1970s I served for a time as pastor of Washington, D.C., First Church of the Nazarene—then a white congregation struggling with the need to minister to its African-American neighbors in the nation's first major city with a majority Black population. A Nazarene pastor of African descent from Guyana happened by to visit. I learned later that his son was a student at Howard University in Washington, D.C. Rev. Carleton Helliger expressed his interest in attending the church and eventually bringing his wife and younger children to the United States. His happened to be the second immigrant family our family had the privilege of greeting as they entered the United States through Washington National Airport.

While the congregation at that time was entirely white and not sure about opening its membership to minority people, it could hardly resist this ordained Nazarene pastor from Guyana. I had the privilege of receiving him and his family into membership, the first minorities to join. They helped change the face of that congregation. In time, Washington First Church became a growing, international, multicultural congregation reaching out to its neighbors living nearby as well as those who drive for miles to be a part of an inclusive congregation. We didn't talk about it then, but as I look back, I see Rev. Helliger was a missionary of sorts in Washington, D.C., who helped us expand our mission to include not only an immigrant family but also our minority neighbors too long excluded from our worship and fellowship.

Some of the changes within the church are inevitable. The world and thus the church are changing so quickly it's hard to keep up. However, the most important changes will need to be intentional if the church is to take full advantage of the new opportunities to fulfill its mission. This book will attempt to describe the changes that are occurring and those that need to occur. While the title is *The Changing Face of the Church,* in part the book is about changing the face of the *American* church.

1

The Diversity Advantage
Church Leaders Call for Change

THE DRAMATIC GROWTH THE CHURCH OF THE NAZARENE has experienced in its mission fields may be about to occur in the United States if the American church is able to take advantage of the evangelism and the new church opportunities among both the immigrant and historic minorities.

Business communities are beginning to see these demographic changes as the "diversity advantage." In the global economy, the United States is seen by corporate leaders to have a competitive edge because of its diverse population. If, for instance, a company seeks to enter a foreign market, it can draw upon Americans from almost any cultural, national, or language group to build a bridge to developing profitable contacts. Even within the United States and Canada, corporations are finding it advantageous to include minorities and women in the workplace. As older markets are saturated, opportunities for expansion are found most often in specialized cultural and language minority groups. To take advantage of these market opportunities, businesses find it to their advantage to work with and through minorities.

The Multicultural Ministries office was created in 1995

to help the Church of the Nazarene in the United States and Canada take advantage of the opportunities to extend its ministries among the minority groups. The message from church leaders is that minorities are both welcomed and needed to help the church accomplish its mission. Furthermore, minority groups and their leaders will be included in the decision-making processes and leadership structures of the church.

John A. Knight, general superintendent, and Bill M. Sullivan, Church Growth Division director, addressed a Multicultural Ministries committee February 4, 1995. This committee was convened to address the need for denominational leaders to make those changes necessary to take advantage of this new opportunity for evangelism among minorities.[1] As Dr. Knight said, "We see more change in one year than our forebears saw in a lifetime." He went on to observe that with the dramatic social changes engulfing us all, "our field of evangelism has changed and will continue to change in the foreseeable future."

Dr. Sullivan, an acknowledged expert in the church growth movement, claims that "if the Church of the Nazarene is to play anything like a significant role in the 21st century, we must change the cultural makeup of this denomination we love and cherish. . . . If we hope to be representative of the American population, then we must increase the percentage of minorities 40 percent in the next 50 years!" He goes on to stress the urgency of the needed change: "The Church of the Nazarene will rise to the challenge, or it will falter, flounder, fail, and fade."

The key thoughts of the February 1995 committee meeting were summarized in a brochure titled *Diversity Leadership in the Church of the Nazarene.*[2] The presentations that follow clearly set the course. These statements and the summary included in the brochure make it clear that the intention of the Church of the Nazarene is to reach every language and cultural group within the borders of the

United States and Canada, just as it seeks to extend its ministry around the world.

CALL TO ACTION
John A. Knight

It is a special joy to be here with you today to discuss ways we as a church can better carry out the Great Commission and to respond faithfully and effectively to the variety of people groups in our society. Secondarily, we hope to assist Dr. Tom Nees, director of Multicultural Ministries, in accomplishing his goals. He, of course, has invited you here because of your insight, expertise, experience, background, knowledge, and churchmanship. A quick glance around the circle reveals that a blue-ribbon group of personnel has been assembled. I commend Dr. Nees for his good judgment in selection and also you for responding to his invitation.

What he has labeled "Call to Action" on our agenda, I am simply taking as an opportunity to welcome you to our dialogue today and to express appreciation for your assistance in a most important and crucial area of the church's life and ministry. I am certain that I express the feeling of the Board of General Superintendents in affirming Dr. Nees and you as we search for new and better and perhaps speedier ways to minister to the plethora of cultural and racial backgrounds found in America today, and to involve these persons in the life and growth of the Church of the Nazarene. This endeavor cannot be delayed or postponed in the light of the rapid and continuing changes taking place in our society.

Someone has suggested that we see more change in one year than our forebears saw in a lifetime. At least the pace of change has dramatically increased in our time. More often than not, the pivotal changes do not occur because we scheduled them but result from the interaction of many factors that we do not foresee and cannot control. No one planned the Protestant Reformation, the discovery of the two continents west of Europe and Africa, the slaughter that two world wars turned out to be, or the collapse of the Soviet Union. The winds of history blow as they will, bringing the unexpected to pass and summoning us to adjust our sails as best we can. So, too, no one planned the relentless and irreversible pluralization of the American populace, which is taking us ever farther from the Puritan goal of the kingdom of God in America—in my view a mixed blessing.

Despite the steady pluralization that began in the 19th century, until recently the ethos of the nation was shaped by Protestantism, especially by the mainliners who "felt responsible for America: for its moral structure, for the religious content of national ideals, for the education and welfare functions that government would not (or, it was thought, should not) carry out."[3]

Whether we feel guilty of nostalgia, that era cannot be restored. Twenty years ago Sydney Ahlstrom observed that "only in the 1960s would it become apparent that the Great Puritan epoch in American history had come to an end."[4] Declaring the death of Protestant dominance may be premature. Many liberal Protestants have rarely felt good about their real achievements because their originally religiously motivated institutions later "belonged no longer to the saints but to the citizenry," prompting prophets to cry that "the success of the church signaled the failure of the gospel."[5]

In any case, according to Leander E. Keck, distinguished New Testament scholar, "one reason there is chaos in the churches and confusion in the land is that while the Puritan era may have ended, the Puritan idea continues in the determination to Christianize America."[6]

The main point to be made here is that in ever larger areas of our country, the Protestant—indeed the Christian—franchise has expired; it will not be renewed. Only tyranny can restore it. The future is less and less like the past.

The whole picture is made even more complicated by a surge of new immigrants and new babies, so that the population of the United States is growing much faster than earlier projected. The Census Bureau forecasts that the population will reach 275 million in the year 2000 and 383 million in 2050. That amounts to an increase of 50 percent in six decades. The change is striking and dramatic.

Cultural, governmental, familial, and religious ideas and ideals are altering the earlier pervasive corpus of Christian teachings. The Census Bureau now estimates that 200,000 undocumented immigrants will arrive each year for 60 years. Legal and illegal immigration combined will increase the population by an average of 880,000 a year for the next six decades. The annual increase could be as high as 1.4 million.

Various groups have grown within the population as follows: Black—13.2 percent; Native American—37.9 percent; Asian-Pacific Islanders (including Chinese, Filipino, Japanese, Asian Indian, Korean, Vietnamese, Hawaiian, Samoan, Guamanian)—107.8 percent; Hispanic (Mexican, Puerto Rican, Cuban, and others)—53 percent.

These changes in racial mix are not cited to decry or to evaluate them as either good or bad. They are simply statistical ways of reminding us that our field of evangelism has changed and will continue to change in the foreseeable future. These people respond to the gospel and to Christ and the church best early on after entering their new society.

The strategies that may need to be developed in order to reach these minority groups with the gospel may arise in part out of our discussion today as we think about dealing with change and working creatively with diversity. I am not here to suggest what carrying out our mission would entail in this kind of setting nor how it should be carried out.

Several things, however, can be done that may or may not seem obvious:

● Improve present efforts in training minority leaders.

● Show leaders how to equip the laity in doing the work of the church.

● Encourage strong minority pastoral leadership, and reward development.

● Assist each Multicultural Ministries strategy committee in designing outreach events and programming for clearly defined groups of people—aimed at a specific audience.

● Continue to establish preaching points and plant churches.

I believe our goal is that one-third of the new church plants until 2000 will be among minority groups. The National Black Strategy Committee has set several goals, including this one—each region in the United States will plant at least one new Black church each year through 2000. There should be 103 fully organized Black Churches of the Nazarene in the United States at that time.

Other strategy committees are formulating their own goals.

What a privilege is ours in seeking to find ways to glorify Christ and to introduce Him as "the world's only Savior"! He died for all people everywhere, whatever their racial, ethnic, linguistic, religious, or social background. Not only is this our privilege, but also it is our responsibility as faithful stewards of the gospel of Christ. Thus we are "called to action," not only by the church, but by Christ himself.

This group is free to pursue these ends with the full blessing of the whole church, focusing on the unity within the Body of Christ while at the same time recognizing and appreciating the diversity of Christ's Body. My prayer, like yours, is that the Holy Spirit will guide our thought processes and our conversations as we work in Jesus' name and for His glory.

PREPARING TO CHANGE
BILL M. SULLIVAN

In an interview with *Parade Magazine* regarding his book *The Road Ahead*, Bill Gates, personal computer software guru and the richest man in America, said, "It's pretty hard to be successful if all you're doing is thinking about some business goal. It's a lot easier if you pick something you bring a passion to."*

Along with the business world, the Church has, for the past decade or two, prepared for the future by developing mission statements, key and critical objectives, programs, evaluations, plans "B," et cetera, et cetera—all of which are very good.

It isn't that there is anything negative about all this management by objective process. It's just that it is so difficult. Perhaps Bill Gates is right—it's a lot easier if we choose objectives about which we are passionate.

I've been thinking a lot recently about the Church

---

*Lyric Wallwork Winik, "Our Strength Is That We Embrace Change," *Parade Magazine,* January 28, 1996, 15. Reprinted with permission from *Parade*, copyright © 1996.

of the Nazarene in the 21st century. Will we be a church for the new times? Will we play as significant a role in the 21st century as our Holiness pioneers played in the 20th? The answer may depend not so much on rational processes and logistical planning as it does on passion.

Will we bring a passion to the 21st century? If so, what will it be?

Frankly, I'm increasingly going back to my roots. Although my grandfather joined the Church of the Nazarene very early in the century, and my father was a member of the church most of his life, I never really attended church until I was 12 years old. It was in my very first Vacation Bible School, when the theme was on Jesus' words "Follow me," that I was first converted. Three years later I heard Jesus say, "Follow me, and I will make you fishers of men" (Matt. 4:19).

Now, almost half a century later, I'm about to come to the conclusion that being a fisher of men was all the Lord really had in mind for me to do. Don't misunderstand me. It takes a lot of preparation, skill, and persistence to be a good fisher of men. And, in some respects, I've become a sort of commercial fisherman—selling boats and fishing equipment to hands-on fishermen. But still it's the catch that really matters.

Recently I walked along a Pacific Ocean beach in Peru, South America, with missionary Al Swain. All along the beach there were 35- to 50-foot fishing boats. Sitting cross-legged were hundreds of fishermen mending their nets. Offshore a half mile were many other boats just waiting to launch out the moment they received the news that the fishing was good.

Just a short distance from there, in the village of Monsefu, we visited the first Nazarene mission station, established by Roger Winans. Here is where the Church of the Nazarene began its fishing-for-men operation in Peru. Now, 1 in 20 Churches of the Nazarene in the whole world is located in Peru! They have always known in Peru that fishing for men (that is, winning people to Christ) was their primary business. It wasn't a goal—it was a passion!

Will the Church of the Nazarene bring an evangelistic passion to the 21st century in North America? Will we? Can we? That is the real question. For, you see, we can bring to the 21st century only the passion we have. And it will be our passion that determines what the Church of the Nazarene is and does in the 21st century.

If the Church of the Nazarene is to play anything like a significant role in the 21st century, we must change the cultural makeup of this denomination we love and cherish.

Currently in America there are 25 to 30 million African-Americans, 25 to 30 million Hispanics, and another 25 to 30 million people from a variety of cultures. That is close to one-third of the total population. By the middle of the next century it will be one-half of the population.

Currently in the U.S.A. Church of the Nazarene, only about 10 percent is minority. If we hope to be representative of the American population, then we must increase the percentage of minorities 40 percent in the next 50 years!

If the challenge were only numerical, that would be one thing. But such a numerical increase must inevitably bring concomitant changes in attitude, understanding and flexibility, organization, and who knows what else. One thing is certain: there must be dramatic changes in the future—that is, if the church is to have a significant future.

The diversity of our nation has become so great that we can no longer compartmentalize it. Patronizing is not an option. Symbolic inclusion is laughable. English-speaking Whites, even with all of the money, no longer own the territory. It's a multicultural world, and Whites will simply have to get with the program.

I know that this is difficult to believe, and, of course, there will probably always be exceptions. Here and there pockets of early Americana will continue to exist, but not in the major population concentrations. The church is called to minister where the people are, and that means the urban areas. And in the urban sprawl, all across the nation, monumental social changes will occur.

The Church of the Nazarene will rise to the challenge, or it will falter, flounder, fail, and fade. None of us wants to see the church marginalized in the future. That's why we are here today. We all believe that God wants us to be a redemptive fellowship committed to holistic evangelism.

That is not likely to happen unless we bring a passion to the mission of designing a new future for the Church of the Nazarene. Our challenge is not novel speculation. It is daring to surrender, to close the book—not on the final chapter, but on a previous volume—and then open the next volume on an unbelievable future.

But Bill Gates is probably right—success is more a matter of passion than it is the pursuit of a goal. And so preparing to change means identifying leaders who are passionate about the commitments necessary for the future we are facing. That may sound simplistic. It sounds scary to me. It is not a method I would desire. But it is probably the only effective one.

I'm not sure we will choose it. I'm not sure we have the courage to choose such an option. But it is a promising opportunity in which God has given us the privilege of choice.

2

Who Are We?

A Heartland Church Redefined

*I*N HIS BOOK *WHO WE ARE*, URBAN AFFAIRS COLUMNIST SAM Roberts of the *New York Times* offers what is described on the book's cover as "a portrait of America based on the latest U.S. Census." The United States Constitution requires that every 10 years a census be taken, not just to find out how many of us there are, but to inquire into all sorts of things, creating enough information to fill many books and to make *Who We Are* a fascinating read. In an early paragraph, Roberts recounts a statement from historian Theodore H. White that "America is more of an idea than a place." This "idea," says Roberts, has "drawn together the most diverse population on earth and one that is becoming more varied every day."

The "average American" by census statistics is "a 32.7-year-old white woman who lives in a mortgaged suburban three bedroom home, heated by natural gas. She is a married mother, with some German ancestry, on the cusp of the MTV generation—roughly the 13th to come of age since Benjamin Franklin's. She graduated from high school and holds a clerical job. She moves to a new home more frequently than residents of any other developed nation. She is also a myth."[1]

Just as the mythical "average American" doesn't exist, neither is there such a thing as an "average American Nazarene." With the wealth of information provided by the 1990 census, Roberts could accurately describe who we are as Americans, and by comparing this with past data and updated information, he can make projections about who we will be in the future. We are at a distinct disadvantage with church demographics.

Unlike the United States census, there is no Nazarene census. Most of what is known is based on the reports pastors send to their districts each year. From these reports the church counts members and their involvement in various church activities. For instance, the Sunday School breakdown gives us some information about the age groupings, from which we can estimate the average age of Nazarenes. A good deal is known about pastors from ordination records, but virtually nothing official is known about lay members. The income of Nazarenes can be estimated by looking at the total giving record of a particular congregation. The racial and cultural identity of the denomination is projected from information pastors submit, identifying the major groups represented in the community and within the congregation. While there are records identifying minority congregations, this information is voluntarily offered for purposes of affiliation rather than statistical accuracy. As an example, the number of members in churches identified as African-American is known, but there is no information about how many non-African-Americans attend these churches or how many African-Americans attend churches with other cultural or racial descriptions. There are no church records identifying the racial identity of pastors or lay members.

From what we know, the mythical average American Nazarene would most certainly be a white woman, of about the same income and slightly older than the national average, and most likely living in a small town or suburban midwestern neighborhood. Demographer and futurist Russ Bredholt Jr. has served as an adviser to various departments of the General Board for the past 17 years. His observation is that the Church of the Nazarene, along with many other denominations, has to deal with the aging of its membership. "Organizations like people are mortal. However, unlike people, organizations (such as the church) don't have to die. The problem lies not with aging itself. Rather, the real problem stems from failing to retain younger members and from seeking new people for Christ in an ongoing way."

According to Dale Jones, administrative director of the Church Growth Research Center, the Church of the Nazarene "has more churches in more counties in the United States than all but seven other denominations."[2] He says, "We've done a good job of reaching lots of America, but it's not been urban America." The heaviest concentration of Nazarenes can be found in several midwestern states concentrated around Illinois, Indiana, and Ohio. Even though the earliest beginnings of the church can be traced to southern California, the Southeast, and the Northeast, according to Timothy Smith in volume 1 of *Called unto Holiness*, the Church of the Nazarene has become a "heartland" church.

For a relatively small denomination to cover so much territory, it comes as no surprise that Nazarenes have become a denomination of commuters. When asked to describe their current situations, pastors often talk about the distance between the church and where the parishioners live. Members of the Church of the Nazarene did in the past 30 years what others decided to do. They left the old neighborhoods of the city and moved to the suburbs. In order to maintain their original church connections, some are forced to drive great distances to attend services. The people relocated, but the church property remained. The potential problem lies in replacing the community members with a new generation who will most likely come from racially diverse neighborhoods nearby. It means starting over. These stories from pastors can be translated into denominational trends, according to Dale Jones: "The trends are that the white English-speaking churches are not being replaced. They are older congregations. Generally we've had a decline in church planting since the late '50s. We had a bit of an upturn in the '80s, but it's leveled off and, in fact, seems to be declining again to the point where we have fewer active English-speaking, predominately white congregations today than we had 10 years ago, and it's been declining most years in the '90s. That cannot continue to go on indefinitely without there being a decline in the membership and attendance figures and the voting strength in our district assemblies. At the same time, we've been having great results among some of the other groups, notably the Hispanics."

Further evidence of this trend can be found in Gallup surveys of future church attendance. The greatest potential, according to studies, will be among Hispanics and African-Americans. These two groups are much more likely to become a part of a congregation than any other cultural category.

According to Bredholt, mission and ministry opportunities are found both inside the current congregation and outside in the communities where we are located. "Someone once said that the best way to hide something is to put it in plain view. This may be the situation facing many churches. A congregation's future is directly related to its ability to make a meaningful connection with households that are nearby." Dealing with this situation, according to Bredholt, has to do with an understanding of geography and demography. "According to the Census Bureau, 61 percent of the Hispanics in the U.S.A. can be found in just three states: California, Texas, and Florida." Therefore the best opportunities for reaching certain groups will depend on where you live.

Renewal and revitalization often occur first on the boundaries with those closest to the changes in society and culture. The question becomes: How will the Church of the Nazarene respond to this kind of change? Some encouraging signs are coming from the district superintendents in the United States and Canada. In a recent Leadership Development Program in Boston, the superintendents were challenged with the idea of pursuing evangelistic opportunity, even if it means taking some calculated risks and thinking outside current structure. The Church of the Nazarene began with a certain flexibility as a part of its character and personality. It will need to recover some of that flexibility in order to deal with a changing world.

It may be that the greatest challenge to the "average Nazarene" is to accept the fact that some of the accepted ways of doing things are, in fact, cultural and not necessarily essential to either the gospel or the Church of the Nazarene. It was not too long ago that some among us were willing to stake their faith on the King James Version of the Bible. What could be more culturally biased than an English translation of the Bible named after a monarch who was not particularly pious? Many, if not most, of our religious ceremonies and hymns are of European origin from the 18th and 19th centuries. This is not bad, unless it becomes the standard by which others are judged.

As a group, American Nazarenes are a predominately white, heartland church. The church's strength is in the commitment of its members to attend church regularly and resist self-destructive behavior. When rightly proclaimed, the church offers the world a faith that is optimistic about the possibilities of personal and social transformation. The denomination has been more generous in giving than most. It has been motivated by a global vision of a church spreading to all the nations.

The new challenge is to allow this tradition to lead through the changes brought on by cultural pluralism and urbanization. With the urbanization of society, the church will need to move from a concentration of town-and-country ministries to urban ministries. With the aging of society, the graying of America, an aging membership will be stretched to retain flexibility, seeking the input and involvement of the next generation, without which there is no future. And with the browning of America, the English-speaking white majority will have to learn to be comfortable in its new role as one minority group among others. It's not enough to just tolerate or put up with cultural differences. In an international, multicultural church, each Nazarene minister and member will need to become a global Christian.

Just as Theodore White said that America is more an idea than a place, the Church of the Nazarene is more a family than an organization. Strict loyalty to organizational democratic majority rule may not serve this growing, culturally diverse family. In order for the Church of the Nazarene to expand into new areas, there will have to be intentionality by those in positions of authority to ensure the emergence of minority leaders among both clergy and laity.

Putting aside the idea of change for the sake of change, it is important to remember that opportunities never stay around very long. When they present themselves, leadership has to move. Our evangelization efforts must include ethnic and minority populations. The system and structure may need to be realigned in order for this to happen.

As general secretary and the chief operating officer of Nazarene Headquarters in Kansas City, Jack Stone is at the center of the Nazarene organizational structures. He believes that if the church is to reach the pluralistic societies of the United States and Canada as well as continue to extend itself around the world, the work of the "International Center," as headquarters is often called, must make a dramatic change. When asked if the church should look like America, he replied, "I really don't know. I think we have to reflect the culture we're in, but we also have to reflect the church we're part of. I told an associate once, 'Don't destroy what we have to make this church become what it should become.' So I think that is the challenge, the tension we face. We can't destroy what we have in order to force the church into some kind of artificial balance. I think we have to move toward the demographic reality. I'd rather see carefully laid-out strategies that people can buy into regardless of their culture—recognizing the diversity of our country and the nations of the world and that these changes need to occur—and then allowing them to happen."

Stone believes that the church has "roomy beliefs," that it's theologically flexible enough to take advantage of the new opportunities for evangelism in a pluralistic society. He says, "I don't want to be labeled a liberal or a conservative, either one, because I think the Church of the Nazarene is very—well, from the Evangelical sense—moderate in its position. You know, the Articles of Faith were written very roomy. When you talk about eschatology, when you talk about the Atonement, when you talk about baptism, when you talk about the inspiration of the Scriptures—the Articles of Faith are very roomy. A lot of Nazarenes don't recognize that, I think, particularly heartland Nazarenes. But we shouldn't be quibbling over hairline interpretations of theology."

Stone believes, and others agree with him, that Nazarene "roomy" doctrinal flexibility is not matched by organizational flexibility. He says, "Structurally we have to change, we will change, because membership is changing. But the question in my mind that I'm not thoroughly convinced of is 'Can we intentionally strategize organizational change?' I don't know how to do that for sure, but we need to look at those things."

One of the first things he would change is the divisional structures at Nazarene Headquarters that tend to divide the church operations between the United States/Canada and the rest of the world. "I think this center that we're working in, that we're a part of, must globalize. Eighty percent of what we do now is the United States. I think it needs to be flip-flopped. We really need to focus globally. And every entity, I think, has to be hooked into the global church. If we don't, then I think we'll be an entity that won't relate to the changing face of the church. And I think that once we globalize—that doesn't mean we don't include the United States and Canada—we become an inclusive international center. Just to put it bluntly, I think we need to do away with divisional walls. We need to be a center that is focused on the mission of the church globally. And to do that, we develop clusters rather than divisions."

Stone would go farther by implementing recommendations from the Commission on the International Church to remove from the *Manual* "a lot of the organization trapping that is purely American and make the *Manual* more an international global document without all the culturalism from America." When asked about the cultural dimensions of worship, Stone responded, "Yes, then I think our worship, I think our style, I think our traditions that we hold so dear are not necessarily adaptable to diverse groups. I think a lot of us in the United States, in the Midwest and other areas, need to understand that the church is much broader, much more diverse."

When asked how all these changes sound to "heartland Nazarenes," Stone answered very personally: "Well, I don't know. I don't know for sure how well it's going to be received totally, but I think it's a reality we face. I'm 58 years old, and I think having lived and worked in the center of the United States largely—well, the Southeast and so on—I'm influenced by American culture and the American church. But I've also, quite naturally, had exposure to all the regions of the world, preached in many of them, and been a part of those cultures. I think our heart for evangelism and world missions will make this easier for the heartland churches. And I think the changing membership of the church, the changing representation of the church, will give importance to issues besides the ones we thought were important in the past. I think there will be a great move toward an inclusive church."

If Stone is uncertain about how these necessary changes will occur, he is also hopeful that heartland Nazarenes will do the right thing. He said, "You know, we can talk about being an international church the rest of our lives, but we have to demonstrate inclusivity, not exclusivity. And for the Midwesterner, maybe, and some others in the church—I'm just focusing here because I know this part of the world—I think carefully laid-out intentional strategies that are inclusive will be well received. I have that confidence."

During the September 1995 Leadership Conference for United States and Canadian Nazarene district superintendents, church consultant Kennon Callahan presented church leaders with studies indicating that when unchurched people look for a church home, they are seeking two things: compassion and community. Too often, he said, when pastors and other church leaders seek to expand, they emphasize programs and promotion. He went on to say that the church needs to understand the questions those outside the faith community are asking. They want to know the answer to these questions: "Does anyone care?" and "Do I belong?" How the church answers those two questions will determine what the church will become in the 21st century.`

3

Minority Ministries in the American Church

Growth and Change Among Historic and Immigrant Minorities

IN HIS KEYNOTE ADDRESS TO THE SEPTEMBER 1994 MULTICUL-
tural Ministries Conference in Nashville, General Superintendent Paul Cunningham took a bold step in setting the
agenda for the Nazarene commitment to include minority
people in the life of the church.

He told the audience of this first official gathering of
minority groups within the church that this was "one of the
most exciting chapters in the history of the Church of the
Nazarene." Before a culturally diverse audience of leaders
and delegations from the 17 strategy committees organized
and supported by the Church Growth Division, Dr. Cunningham recalled his first exposure to racial conflict as a
boy growing up in Chicago. He learned early the value of
cross-cultural friendship. Caught in the crossfire of gang
conflicts among ethnic Whites, Hispanics, and Blacks, his
protector and friend was Moses Washington, a Black ama-
teur boxer. He remembered how his [Cunningham's] mother led their Black mail carrier to the Lord—a man who was

later to become pastor of a large African-American congregation. Cunningham chose as his theme "There's Room at God's Table for Everyone," urging the church to practice the kind of acceptance he learned as a boy in his own home.

It was when a church in his home city, Chicago First, was forced to sell its property that Cunningham said he became concerned for the future of the church among minorities in the cities. "I suppose that's why I was so concerned as a young man when I saw our churches abandoning the cities. I was a seminary student, and Chicago First Church was valiantly trying to stay in a changing neighborhood, but they weren't being very successful with it, and finally out of financial necessity decided to relocate."

Cunningham recounted that back then he advocated a partnership of some kind among local, district, and general leaders to prevent the sale and loss of these properties. He predicted what has now come true. The church is now trying to reenter these neighborhoods, but properties sold cheaply then are now unaffordable.

"Someday," said Cunningham, "we're going to get a vision for the cities" with their concentration of minority groups, their cultural diversity, and their variety of languages. "It's missionary work in our cities. We'll not save our cities until we get a missionary vision for our cities." He went farther: "We left the cities, and then the new America moved to the cities. The mission field decided to come to us, and it came to stay."

In calling for a partnership to provide a way to retain properties when local congregations choose to relocate and to understand cities as mission fields, he challenged much of the conventional thinking regarding congregational development. Relocating congregations have seen their transitions as the natural counterpart of the upward mobility of their members. The success of the moving congregation has traditionally been seen in its capacity to move to a better neighborhood, transferring its equity in property from an older building in a changing neighborhood. While this may be expedient for a local congregation, from the larger perspective of a denominational vision for the cities it has proven to be counterproductive. Cunningham's idea of a partnership is a bold call for cooperation, for finding a way of retaining strategic properties when members and congregations relocate.

Even more far-reaching is Cunningham's description of cities as the "mission fields" come to America and his call for "missionary work" and "missionary vision." As noted earlier, Jerry Appleby sounded this theme in his 1986 book *Missions Have Come Home to America.* It's one thing, however, to notice that cities have become as foreign to mainstream, heartland America as any foreign country; it is something more for a church leader to call for new definitions of mission and new strategies and structures for ministry among and through minorities in these cities.

As he looked out upon a culturally diverse audience enjoying worship and praise in their several different languages, he observed that "celebrating diversity is so much better than creating barriers to mutual understanding"; but he went on to warn, "We must remember, as we work together celebrating diversity, that discrimination, prejudice, domination in all cases is a sin issue." He said that it is when diversity results in conflict that the Wesleyan-Holiness message of "holiness of heart and life" makes a difference. "The sound of prejudice and disharmony is in the carnal nature."

If the Holiness churches have been slow to confront the racism that leads to exclusion and separatism, on this occasion Cunningham sought to emphasize the diversity advantage. "I believe cultural diversity is providing us with one of the greatest opportunities the church has ever had, because we have the message that enables us to live together and enjoy each other at God's table. That is what our message does for us. You can't hate somebody and have holiness of heart and life; you can't discriminate against somebody and have holiness of heart and life. The two do not go together, you see. They just don't go together."

He recognized that near the 21st century it's too late for minorities to be standing in line waiting for the opportunity to serve and lead. He assured the diverse delegates and friends of the convention, "There's room in the Church of the Nazarene for everyone." To their sustained applause he added, "You don't have to elbow your way in to the table. We want to set a place for you. You're invited. There's room at God's table for everyone."

This Multicultural Ministries Convention was the result of steps initiated in 1986 under the direction of Michael Estep, then the Church Extension Ministries director within the Church Growth Division. The Church Growth Division has responsibility for giving support to minority ministries from the former Home Missions Department. Previously, when Raymond Hurn was Home Missions director, several leaders, including Jerry Appleby, Franklin Cook, Roger Bowman, and Bill Young, were assigned to this task. Estep organized minority strategy committees for each racial or language minority group with an identifiable presence in the Church of the Nazarene. This was the most recent denominational effort to recognize and link people of similar cultural identities. Recognition and support for minority groups has been evolving due to changing circumstances both inside and outside the church. The all-Black Gulf Central District and its training center at Institute, West Virginia, was dissolved in 1968 due to sensitivities following the Civil Rights Movement. Black congregations were assimilated into regular predominately white districts. In January 1969, the Board of General Superintendents met with Warren A. Rogers, Gulf Central district superintendent; Raymond Hurn, Home Missions director; and white district superintendents affected by the integration move of the 1968 General Assembly. These superintendents agreed to visit the Black pastors and personally welcome them to their districts. Hurn remembers this as a "frightfully difficult time." He says, however, the Black pastors "were warmly welcomed, and some soon were serving on District Advisory Boards."

In 1976 Spanish-speaking and American Indian districts administered by the Department of Foreign Missions were turned over to the Department of Home Missions. Following its organization in 1948, the Department of Home Missions began to pioneer work outside the United States in English-speaking countries as well as in European countries similar to the majority, northern European population in the United States. Organizing strategy committees extended official denominational efforts to give attention to and support for the full range of minority leaders and groups.

Estep called attention to the steady, if not dramatic, growth of minority works—organized churches, church-type missions, and Bible studies: 183 in 1970, 270 in 1980, 651 in 1990, and by the time of the Multicultural Ministries Conference in 1994 there were 785 identifiable minority works. These works accounted for 34,000 Nazarene members, 50,000 enrolled in Sunday School, and combined annual giving of $13 million. By 1995 the 10 to 15 percent minority members (with financial support and encouragement from the majority white church) of the Church of the Nazarene had started more new churches than the 90 percent English-speaking white majority.[1] In fact, in 1995 there were more new Spanish-speaking congregations started (14) than English-speaking white. (See Appendix 1 for charts and statistics of minorities and strategy committees.)

Estep described the apostle Paul as a bicultural model for Multicultural Ministries. He said, "No one in ministry today, no matter of what ethnic group, can afford to be one culture only. We will have to adjust to those around us."

In 1995 Hispanics were the largest and fastest-growing minority group in the church. The traditional strength of the Hispanic work has been on the organized Spanish mission districts. However, in recent years the most rapid increase in new churches has been on predominately white districts. Much of the visibility, if not the growth, of Hispanic ministries can be accredited to Publications International, a division of the Nazarene Publishing House, providing high visibility for a few Hispanic leaders at the center of Nazarene Headquarters. The presence of these leaders translating Spanish literature provides a centralized denominational base for Hispanic leadership.

José Pacheco, chairman of the Hispanic Strategy Committee and administrative coordinator for Hispanic Publications, was born and raised in a Nazarene home in Monterrey, Mexico. He began his ministry in various mission projects in Mexico City before coming to Kansas City in 1974 to join H. T. Reza, director of Spanish Publications. He noted that before he arrived, the Spanish work in the United States was done primarily through the Spanish districts. "Now all that has changed," he said. "I have seen a tremendous change in how the Hispanics are being reached by all the districts, all the churches, all over, even in Alaska and Hawaii. I have seen that little by little the Anglo- or English-speaking white churches are aware that the Hispanics now are officially the second-largest minority. I have always said that we are the first, if you count undocumented immigrants. I feel very happy that somebody's trying to reach the Hispanics besides these Spanish districts."

Pacheco noted that when the English-speaking white districts began starting Hispanic churches, the Spanish districts were very reluctant to cooperate. He said, "They felt that they were being invaded in their territory of expertise. But as recently as the last three or four years, that has changed. I have seen a very good change of attitude on our Spanish districts toward the Anglo districts. I venture to say that they are looking for ways to cooperate to see how we can reach the Hispanics with whatever means we have."

When asked whether in the light of the growth of Hispanics on the English-speaking white districts there is still a reason for Spanish (or, Latin) districts, Pacheco contended for the important place of these minority districts, even though in the future they may not continue in their present form. He said, "I think the three districts that we have now, maybe in two, three, or four more years will need to change. But for now I think they have a reason to exist. Not everybody in these churches will be happy to integrate with the Anglo districts, and the end result will be that we will lose them."

Even though the Spanish districts and culturally specific Spanish-speaking congregations on majority districts attract most of the Hispanic Nazarenes, Pacheco is of the opinion that cultural assimilation will sooner or later bring people together. He said, "The English-speaking white churches, I think, are ready now to assimilate our people." His advice to pastors: "If you are trying to reach the newly arrived Hispanics, you need somebody who speaks Spanish. But if you want to reach the second and third generation of Hispanics, you don't need to do anything different. All you need to do is just reach out to them, and they will feel welcome, integrated into the Anglo church."

It may surprise some in the majority white church community to realize that Hispanics are often looking to churches as a gateway into the larger society. "In the case of the newly arrived," Pacheco says, "maybe you need to open the door for some kind of assimilation into the culture. They want to be assimilated into this culture. If they stay in the barrio, if they stay just with Hispanics, they will never integrate into this culture. So an English-speaking church will do a great favor to a Hispanic if the church opens the door and helps him or her to integrate into this society. Going to an Anglo church for the Hispanics is a sign of prestige. So the churches should capitalize on that and reach them." Pacheco anticipates 100 new Nazarene Spanish-speaking congregations by 2000, bringing the total to over 250. The only obstacle is the lack of pastors. "We don't have pastors for our new churches, but that's a good problem. That's a very good problem."

The Church of the Nazarene in the United States and Canada has enjoyed rapid growth among groups immigrating from countries where the church has developed through its missionary outreach. Even though the total number of immigrants from countries like Haiti, Korea, and Samoa are relatively small, they have a higher percentage of Nazarenes than the general population of English-speaking whites. This is most obvious with the remarkable growth of Haitian churches in the eastern United States and Canada's Quebec.

Haiti has the most Nazarene members (over 70,000) of any country outside the United States. Haitian Nazarene missions began in 1950 under the leadership of Paul Orjala, the son of immigrants from Finland. The rapid growth of the church in Haiti followed in the wake of missionary work led by various Baptist and Pentecostal groups. In many ways, according to Orjala, the rapid growth of the church in Haiti was a spontaneous movement. Typically an organized church would start several house churches or satellite missions. Only when these missions were ready to become fully organized congregations would they report to the district superintendent, a pattern that was repeated among the first Haitian Nazarene immigrants in south Florida.

In 1964, 15 years after beginning the work in Haiti, Dr. Orjala came to Nazarene Theological Seminary in Kansas City to begin the missiology department. It was a few years later, during the late 1960s, that noticeable numbers of Haitian immigrants began to arrive in the United States and Canada. Among them were Nazarene members, including a few ordained ministers. These first immigrants began meeting in their homes, and, as was their custom, they saw themselves as satellites of their home churches in Haiti and in some instances as satellites of a strong Haitian work that by then had developed in the Bahamas.

Orjala would visit with some of these Haitian immigrants in Miami and later in the New York area. "The first Haitian churches in Miami were not part of any planned movement, and it was not official in any sense," he said. "It was just a spontaneous desire that they felt they ought to do—starting churches in their homes. Eventually some of our Haitian pastors migrated to south Florida. They became pastors of these churches. In other cases, some of the laypeople grew and developed in their leadership ability and became leaders of these churches. They kept contact with Haiti, and we sent them Haitian Sunday School literature—in fact, I often brought back from my trips to Haiti orders of French and Creole books."

The American districts weren't always sure how to respond to or recognize the overnight presence of Haitian Nazarenes, who came in great numbers during the '80s, fleeing—many of them risking their lives traveling by sea in primitive boats—poverty and political oppression. Orjala said, "Probably I am to blame for the informal way in which the Haitians have gotten used to starting churches—just wherever they found a need or if there was a family of Nazarenes that didn't have a church. If it had been in Haiti, they would have contacted their own pastor about it; but since they didn't have a pastor, they didn't exactly know that they should contact a district superintendent. And so there were often a number of Haitian Nazarene churches on some of these Atlantic districts before the district superintendent knew about it. And sometimes when the district superintendents were in a meeting in Kansas City, they would say, 'Hey—your people started a church here, and they didn't get any authorization.' And I would just try to explain to them the kind of spontaneity that had worked in Haiti in connection with the local pastors and our districts. And they would say, 'Well, that's OK. We're glad to have them, but I wish they would let us know what they're doing.'"

There are now more than 50 Haitian congregations in the United States and Canada, with anticipated growth to near 100 churches and missions by 2000. The greatest concentration is in south Florida. One of the largest congregations, North Miami Church of the Nazarene, is led by Pastor Jean Cidel. Rev. Cidel immigrated in 1976. As a boy, he became a Christian through the Church of the Nazarene in Haiti and later studied for the ministry under Dr. Orjala at the Nazarene Bible School in Port-au-Prince.

Rev. Cidel started a Haitian congregation that has grown to over 500, meeting in the property built and maintained until recently by the English-speaking white congregation. When asked how well Haitians are received by the American church, he said, "American people love Haitian people. They love everybody. This church used to be a white church. When they left, they just left the church for us. There was a former member of the white church— many times he passed by here—who would come say to me, 'Brother Cidel, thank you very much, because you kept the church alive where I spent my money.'" He went on to tell of another former member: "There is a woman who comes by to see if the church is still as beautiful as the way she left it. That encourages me. I say to my people, Just keep the church pretty and beautiful. American people are loving people. I know American people. I love American people."

The spontaneous appearance of churches among Haitian immigrants is a story repeated often among Asian and Pacific islanders. In-Gyeong Kim Lundell writes that "Korean churches multiplied like bamboo shoots after the rain."[2] She and her husband, Peter Lundell, are copastors of the Walnut Community Church of the Nazarene on the

Los Angeles District, serving English-speaking and Korean-speaking congregations worshiping in the same building. Both are fluent in Japanese—having served in a mission in Japan—as well as Korean and English. She started the Korean congregation at Los Angeles First Church of the Nazarene. The congregation is now pastored by her brother Sung Dae Kim. In her recently published doctoral missiology dissertation, *Bridging the Gaps: Contextualization Among Korean Nazarene Churches in America,* she describes the struggle of Korean immigrant Nazarenes trying to maintain their faith on American soil. At least for first-generation immigrants, she contends that "Korean people can be Korean Nazarenes, but they cannot be American Nazarenes." She goes on to admit that "second- and third-generation Koreans are still so few that it is difficult to accurately say which direction they will take."[3]

Having served as the Korean coordinator on the Los Angeles District, Kim has developed the theoretical and practical issues of contextualization. Since the largest Korean population outside Korea is now in California, she wants the church to do a better job of understanding and adapting to the Korean worldview. From her own experience she says, "Working with Korean immigrants under American leadership, I encountered an unbridgeable gap between two worldviews, American and Korean."[4] Her study attempts to persuade Nazarenes in the United States to understand that their church is "deeply rooted in the worldview of a particular era of American history."[5] In her view, if the church is to successfully extend itself to minorities in the United States, it must adapt to cultural differences just as it does in its missionary work abroad. The church, she believes, is at a critical moment. If the opportunities for evangelism are to be seized, the church must make room for cultural adaptations without diluting the central theme of the gospel or the mission of the Church of the Nazarene.

In the United States a distinction should be made between immigrant and historic minorities. Immigrants have come by their own free will. Native Americans and Native Canadians are descendants of those whose ancestors predate European expansion and are historic in the truest sense. There are also people of Mexican descent in the southwestern United States whose ancestors claimed territory in New Mexico, Arizona, and California before "the West was won" by settlers from the eastern states. The largest minority group—African-Americans—is also a historic minority (involuntary immigrants), since their ancestors arrived on a slave ship with some of the first English settlers in the 1600s. The African heritage is as important, however tragic and unrecognized, as the European heritage in the forming of American culture.

While there are reasons for talking about minorities in general, care must be taken to understand the differences in the role and relationship of the immigrant groups from those who have been a part of the American culture from the beginning and before. There are no generalizations that fit.

Retired General Superintendent Raymond Hurn traces the beginning of Nazarene consciousness about African-American evangelism in his introduction to *Black Evangelism—Which Way from Here?* (selected messages from the Conference on Urban Ministries in Kansas City, September 14-15, 1973). He recognized that while the church had included other minority groups, "the Black community, which comprises the largest minority in the United States, was not penetrated until recently."[6]

Hurn recounted that the need for the church to reach out and include Blacks was mentioned as early as the 1919 General Assembly. It was in the late 1940s, after the Department of Home Missions was given responsibility for mission work among Blacks, that the first annual conferences of Black leaders were held. Later, in 1953, the Gulf Central District was organized under the direction of a white district superintendent, Leon Chambers. The district included the several states of the Southeast where the majority of African-Americans lived. At the same time another white minister, E. E. Hale, became president of the training center for Black Nazarene ministers in Institute, West Virginia. Dr. Roy F. Smee was the executive secretary of the Department of Home Missions in those pioneer endeavors.

If, as Hurn suggests, the Gulf Central District was formed as an accommodation to Jim Crow segregation, it was disbanded, he notes, as a result of the Civil Rights Movement in the mid-1960s (mentioned earlier). In 1968 the General Assembly took action to disorganize the district and place the 20 Gulf Central churches in the districts of their geographic location. Shortly afterward, by action of the Board of General Superintendents and the recommendation of the board of the West Virginia training center, the school at Institute was merged with Nazarene Bible College. An attempt—for the most part unsuccessful—was made to recruit African-Americans to attend the newly formed Nazarene Bible College in Colorado Springs. Proceeds ($90,000) from the sale of the property at Institute were set aside as the beginning of an endowment for minority students attending Nazarene institutions.

To provide a structure for leadership and fellowship among African-American Nazarenes, several denominationally sponsored committees have been formed, beginning with the Negro Advisory Committee, the Council of Black Churchmen, and now the African-American Strategy Committee. Whatever one thinks about the various denominational efforts to include African-Americans in the life of the church, the reality is that when compared to their numbers in the general population, notwithstanding recent gains, Blacks remain the most underrepresented minority in the church.

The first assembly of the Colored District met January 25, 1948, in Meridian, Mississippi. About the same time Charles Johnson was introduced to the Church of the Nazarene in Orlando, Florida. He eventually found the Lord in a Nazarene revival and in 1996 celebrated 35 years as the pastor of Meridian's Fitkin Memorial Church of the Nazarene, now the largest church on the Mississippi District (over 500 members).

At the age of 12, Johnson was drawn into a youth program in Orlando directed by C. R. Smith, a white furniture salesman and member of Orlando Central Church. He recalls that "C. R. showed me how Christianity should be, because he lived the life." During his teen years, C. R. sponsored a revival campaign to reach out to Blacks in Orlando. Johnson was among the 17 converts who in 1958 organized the first African-American Nazarene church in Florida. He then was encouraged to attend the training center at Institute, which he referred to as "your three years on the desert," a reference to the apostle Paul's sojourn in the desert preparing to preach the gospel.

For Johnson, "Institute," as the training school was called, "was more than just a school. It was a place where you grew up and matured—went through the different phases of your life, plus you learned God's Word." While it wasn't for Blacks only, Black students were especially encouraged by R. W. Cunningham, the saintly Black leader who had become president of Institute. A year before Johnson's graduation in 1960, the nearly empty and run-down Fitkin Memorial Church in Meridian had seen new life under the direction of Roger Bowman, another young African-American pastor, who would become the first African-American to serve as a ministry director at Nazarene Headquarters and who in 1993 became the first African-American to serve as the superintendent of a predominately white district. In 1960, at the request of Gulf Central District Superintendent Warren Rogers, Bowman stayed until Johnson could arrive to take charge of a congregation that then totaled 3 adults and 10 children.

Charles Johnson began his pastorate in Meridian during one of the most tumultuous times in the nation's struggle with race relations. Soon after he entered this ministry, he became a community leader in the struggle for racial justice. He said, "When I came to Meridian, you could not be a Christian and sit around and say, 'Well, let's just praise the Lord in our little corner'—no, no, I believe God wants to help a man physically, spiritually, and financially. I saw beatings; I saw the whole works. I led the protest against different stores where no Blacks were hired. We could spend our money in there, but we couldn't work there; we couldn't even eat at the lunch counters. We had to go over to a corner where the garbage cans were located in order to eat. I knew that wasn't right. As a result, I organized the Meridian Action Committee. Through this committee we broke down the barriers in hiring policies in the stores and the banks, even the telephone company. You just couldn't be a Christian and say, 'God bless you, my child,' when people were out there hungry."

Johnson's church in Meridian has prospered in the post-civil rights era long after the Gulf Central District and the training center at Institute were disbanded. Yet he wonders: "The idea of Institute and the Gulf Central District may have been started by segregationists, but from my viewpoint I saw it as a means to an end to reach Black America. I knew the white community couldn't reach it."

When asked if the maintenance of separate structures doesn't amount to segregation and prejudice, he challenged some popular notions of discrimination. He said, "I think the word 'discrimination' has been misused. I don't discriminate when I have a church full of Black folks. Whites don't discriminate when they come here, and my worship style is not what they want. They go and find what they want. Discrimination is when you set it up to keep me out. We have a choice. Now you have some bigots in the church, but that's not the church. You can go to a white church, and whites can worship with me if that's their worship style."

Even so, Johnson contends that the various committees of and for African-American leaders have not replaced what was lost when Institute and the Gulf Central District were disbanded. The church, in his opinion, must recognize the need for African-American Nazarenes to worship together and identify their own denominational leaders and representatives. This is not, in his view, to create separate structures. It is rather to be effective in reaching people for Christ and the church. He said, "In order to reach Blacks, we've got to have something that Blacks can go to and feel comfortable—gatherings, district assemblies, zone meetings. Black people are going to be reached by Blacks and Black organizations. It's just a way of life. You just have to look at it that way."

The most visible African-American leader in the Church of the Nazarene is Roger Bowman, superintendent of the Los Angeles District, who in 1960 spent a year in Meridian digging out a church that had almost closed its doors for good. His appointment in 1993 and subsequent overwhelming vote of confidence in 1995 by the Los Angeles District Assembly remains the single most hopeful sign among African-American Nazarenes that the Church of the Nazarene is interested not only in evangelizing and starting Black churches but in recognizing and following Black leadership. Serving now as the leader of a diverse district that serves a multicultural population, he sees a challenge facing the church. He said, "Demographic changes are pushing us to train and retrain pastors and the laity to meet the needs of rapidly growing minority populations. It is causing us to refocus and retarget our ministries. We must by deliberate intention seek to win those who are different culturally to Christ and the church, so as to enhance an all-inclusive partnership in ministry. The United States and Canada must also be viewed as a mission field where missionaries are sent and supported. The issue is not primarily culture or color—it is primarily Christian."

As Bowman sees it, the need for more visible minority leadership is critical. "If people cannot identify with the church visually, they are not likely to enter its doors, much less become active members. The church may be open to membership but slow to open its doors to leadership. Where diversity is embraced, the door of ministry is opened wider and becomes an advantage for Kingdom building." In other words, integration must be from the top down rather than from the bottom up.

There is no greater opportunity for the church than among the 40 million African-Americans. African-Americans may be more inclined to the Evangelical faith than the majority English-speaking white population. Even with their tortured history and questions about acceptance within the church, Black Nazarene leaders have continued to serve faithfully and are poised to help the church turn a corner. In his address to the 1973 Conference on Urban Ministries, Bowman said, "I love my church and appreciate the opportunity to serve. Sure, the church has shortcomings. So do I. So do you. But I believe the dawn of a new day is about to break. I can see the church turning the corner."[7] For some the turn has taken too long. Yet leaders such as Roger Bowman and Charles Johnson, whose paths crossed in Meridian, Mississippi, remain hopeful that the same interest to reach African-Americans, which resulted in the organization of the Gulf Central District in Meridian in 1948, will intensify and result in new growth among African-Americans.

The most historic of all the minority groups are the Native American and Native Canadian nations—nations within the nations. Native Americans retain a unique and contradictory place in the culture. They are sometimes revered, as in the naming of sports franchises like the Kansas City Chiefs and Cleveland Indians and in the marketing of tribal artifacts. At other times they are dismissed as primitive, too passive to participate actively in mainstream life, let alone assume places of leadership. It is among Native Americans that the church has seen better success as a percentage of the population than among most other minority groups, including those with significant representation in the Church of the Nazarene.

In 1995 the Navajo District celebrated its 50th anniversary, tracing its beginning to 1945 when Native American churches started by missionaries in Oklahoma and the other southwestern states were organized into the North American Indian District under the jurisdiction of the Department of Foreign Missions. Native American leaders had been trained to start and pastor local churches on reservations as well as in urban areas. It was in 1970 in a mission church in Dilkon, Arizona, in the Navajo Nation, a church pastored by a converted medicine man, that a young couple, Johnny and Juanita Nells, was converted. Johnny and Juanita learned about the Nazarenes through an aunt who had found the Lord in a mission church. His father was a medicine man and had become an alcoholic. A younger sister was critically ill. Through this aunt's prayers, Nells's mother was converted and his sister healed from an illness that, he says, the tribal medical practices were unable to affect.

A chain reaction began. As is so in many minority tribal cultures, the whole family was converted from deeply held and often self-destructive native superstitions, eventually joining a Nazarene mission in the Navajo Nation near Dilkon, Arizona. By the time Nells finished training at the Nazarene Indian Bible College in Albuquerque, New Mexico, and was prepared to begin his pastoral ministry, the district was being led by Julian Gunn, the first Native American district superintendent. In 1985, when the districts were divided, Nells was selected as the Navajo Nation district superintendent, with Gunn leading the Southwest Indian District.

Nells is quick to point out that the spread of Nazarene churches among Native Americans is the direct result of the missionary work begun in the 1940s. Had it not been for the missionaries' labors in training indigenous leadership, his family would not have been introduced to the Church of the Nazarene. Commenting on the importance of this leadership, he quoted one of his own pastors, who said, "It takes a wild horse to catch a wild horse. Any domestic horse will not do." Nells said, "He meant to say that it takes a Native American to reach a Native American."

The growth of the church among Native Americans has been the result of missionary-trained indigenous leadership and the organization of Native American districts that allowed these leaders to be selected to represent their people in denominational events. By comparison, he said, "Other denominations in other Indian nations have looked at the way we have modeled our organization. They covet how we have developed our organization, how we have allowed native leadership to respond. To this very day a lot of other denominations with work among Native Americans are still overseen by missionaries and have not allowed native leadership to take responsibility. The native people are very frustrated because they feel they don't have a representative—they have no one to go to." In his opinion it is these leaders trained and nurtured in Native American Nazarene structures—the two districts and the Nazarene Indian Bible College—who will encourage evangelism and church planting among Native Americans on the regular districts as well as on Native American mission districts.

Nells is as admired for his leadership within his own tribal family in the Navajo Nation as he is respected within the larger church. He serves as the chairman of the Native American Strategy Committee, chairman of the board of Nazarene Indian Bible College and Sun Valley Indian School, and chairman of the Multicultural Council, which includes the leaders of all the minority strategy committees. He is very aware that his place of service and leadership in the church is the result of intentional missionary strategies, which provided structures for leadership as well as training for pastoral service.

Recent immigrants from the Hispanic world, Asia, and the Caribbean account for most of the growth of minorities in the church during the past decade. There have been only slight increases among African-Americans and Native Americans. Among the immigrant groups, the church is unevenly represented, with significant numbers of members and churches from small countries such as Samoa and the Cape Verde Islands. This is the result of immigrants from world areas where the Church of the Nazarene has had active missionary work. The church is well represented among immigrants from countries where missionary work is the strongest.

The church has been successful in many different cultures and world areas when it has set out with a missionary strategy deploying missionaries, providing resources and training, and supporting indigenous leadership. There has been virtually no such sustained effort to reach beyond the English-speaking white majority population in the United States and Canada. The American church has assumed that minority people could and should assimilate with the mainstream styles of worship and organizational structures. Recent increases in minority members and churches have occurred spontaneously, not as the result of a concerted effort to initiate the strategies and make the changes necessary for the church to realize its opportunity in a pluralistic society. While gains among minorities are significant, continued growth will be sustained only as the church becomes an international, multicultural, missionary church in the United States and Canada as it is in other world areas.

4

Building a Multicultural Church

The Changing Boundaries of Community

*I*T IS BECOMING INCREASINGLY CLEAR THAT AS THE FACE OF America has changed, so must the church adapt. The spontaneous growth that generated the greatest increases for the Church of the Nazarene as well as other Evangelical groups in English-speaking white society during the mid-20th century is over. In some parts of the country, churches and districts are struggling just to sustain themselves, let alone expand. At the same time, growth opportunities abound among minorities, particularly recent immigrants who are coming to the United States and Canada in unprecedented numbers. The American church is being called upon to do something new, that is, to include in its fellowship and leadership structures the very people who in the past were the targets of its missionary activity. It won't be easy.

In part, the problem stems from crosscurrents of multiculturalism in society. The struggle within the church mirrors America's struggle, evident in the politics of immigration policy and the campaign to make English the United States' official language. Even as America is becoming more pluralistic, it is becoming more divided. The church will often find itself against society, welcoming the stranger, even providing sanctuary for refugees. The church's base in predictable, stable, predominately white, small-town America is in decline. There are no clear, obvious strategies for church growth in the major metropolitan areas where the combined minority groups already make up the majority.

The church growth movement emerged in the 1960s to provide new directions for evangelism and church planting in America. Unfortunately, in advocating the "homogeneous unit principle," it seemed to promote an expedient way of producing numbers with little concern for the church's prophetic responsibility in secular society. The church cannot be true to its own vision of an international fellowship by dividing into a maze of subcultures, telling people, "If you look like this, or talk like that, we have a place for you." Everyone, regardless of color, culture, or gender, must be welcome in every Nazarene congregation and provided the opportunity to serve and lead if the church is to remain relevant in what some are calling the world's first multicultural society.

The language of the Civil Rights Movement no longer works. Racial and cultural conflicts are not bipolar—Black and White. Few people, even from within the Black community, are putting their lives on the line for integration. They want what everyone else wants—freedom of access to any neighborhood and the opportunity not just to eat at the restaurant lunch counter, but to own the restaurant. The primary issue now is not the cultural or racial makeup of a particular congregation, but whether or not churches provide access and opportunities for anyone and everyone to serve and lead. The critical test now is whether congregations and the church are inclusive or exclusive in their worship and organizational structures. It is becoming clear for the church, as it is within the business community, that if growth is to occur, diversity must be embraced as an opportunity rather than seen as an obstacle. These are the issues to be explored in this chapter.

Not long ago I engaged in surprisingly similar conversations with two Nazarene minority leaders: Julian Gunn, pastor of the First Indian Church of the Nazarene in Albuquerque, New Mexico (also the first Native American to serve as a district superintendent); and Andres Valenzuela, pastor of the First Filipino Church of the Nazarene in Vallejo, California, and chairman of the Filipino Strategy Committee. In a meeting of the Native American Strategy Committee, Dr. Gunn said that his congregation was considering removing the reference to "Indian" from their name because the congregation now includes Hispanics, Whites, and Blacks. Likewise, Rev. Valenzuela has recently said that it is not really accurate to identify his congregation as Filipino, since it has begun to attract a wide variety of people. Both congregations conduct their services in English.

José Pacheco seems to advocate two different if not contradictory strategies to reach Hispanic Americans.[1] On the one hand he understands the need for culturally specific structures to train Hispanic leaders, even supporting the presence of Hispanic districts (or "Latin," as they are known), even though they are an anomaly of sorts, carried over from the days when foreign language ministries in the United States were directed by the Department of Foreign Missions, now the World Mission Division. At the same time, he commends predominately white districts for starting Hispanic churches, assuring the white majority churches that Hispanics will respond positively if they are welcomed into their congregations.

These ideas and strategies parallel the discussion in the African-American community about supporting the historic Black institutions of higher education. Should Black people lend their support to these racially specific colleges and universities or try to get more Blacks in the mainstream universities? The answer is both. In the same way, as the church develops strategies to reflect the pluralism that defines the new face of America, its congregations and denominational structures will be called upon to hold together apparently contradictory ideas.

This is because of two social trends, separatism and assimilation, which, although in opposition, exist side by side in America. Depending on who you listen to, you may be convinced that cultural differences in the United States are so sharply defined that we should replace the idea of the blending of the races and cultures in a "melting pot" with a better metaphor, such as a "stewpot," "salad bowl," or "mosaic," where the cultures interact but retain their individual uniqueness. Others contend that in spite of our differences, we are—at least we are becoming—more alike than we are different.

In spite of these cultural differences, there are some dominant cultural realities that define existence for everyone in America. Culture itself is always evolving. Languages and customs are constantly changing. This is especially so when cultural groups are in close contact and influenced by television and other common sources of information and entertainment.

In his book *Remaking America: How the Benevolent Traditions of Many Cultures Are Transforming Our National Life,* James A. Joseph, an African-American, past director of the Council on Foundations and recently appointed as the United States ambassador to South Africa, describes how the "boundaries of community are changing."[2] In spite of the barriers to community, he contends that "Americans share in a common set of values grounded in at least four principles: (1) that citizens have rights and responsibilities that precede the state and the nation, (2) that society is distinct from government and that government is but one of several sectors that can, and should, promote the common good, (3) that a healthy society is one that protects the freedoms of speech, of the press, of assembly, and of worship, and (4) that the rights of the minority are to be protected by the majority."[3]

The purpose of Joseph's book is to describe the unique contribution made to the charitable interests of American life by African-Americans, Hispanics, Asians, and Native Americans. Each tradition, he writes, is in its own way remaking an America that binds all its people together in a commonly understood social contract. Add to that the overwhelming influence of entertainment, fashion, and the worldwide use of English, and it may be that the "melting pot" metaphor is more descriptive than many want to admit. The Church as well as the nation are caught between two opposing interests: the desire for diversity within unity ("one nation under God") and the wish to retain cultural distinctiveness if not contend for cultural superiority, even if it means keeping foreigners out.

In a discussion following my presentation on multicultural ministries to the summer 1996 Haitian conference in Miami, the pastors debated the importance of retaining Haitian culture and the Creole language. One pastor suggested that if the churches lose the Creole language, they will have lost everything remaining of their identity as a people. Luc Pierre, pastor of the New Jerusalem Church of the Nazarene in Brooklyn, now 20 years in the United States, a graduate of Nazarene Theological Seminary, with a daughter attending Johns Hopkins University on a full scholarship, spoke painfully about his love for Haitian culture and language. Yet he said his children prefer English and have become Americans. He predicted that in another generation, if Haitian Americans intend to keep their own children in the faith, their churches will have to give up some of the Haitian ways that characterize first-generation immigrant churches.

Although In-Gyeong Kim Lundell insists that first-generation Koreans do not want, nor should be expected, to become American Nazarenes, she is not willing to predict that the same will be true for the second and succeeding generations of Korean Americans.[4] In several multicongregational or shared-space ministries such as Los Angeles First Church of the Nazarene, which includes a Korean language congregation (multicongregational Los Angeles First is composed of a federation of four congregations: English-speaking, Spanish, Filipino, and Korean),[5] the trend is for young people from the various congregations to meet together for youth fellowship, while their parents continue to worship with their own language groups.

Charles Johnson, mentioned earlier as the longtime African-American pastor of the Fitkin Memorial Church of the Nazarene in Meridian, Mississippi, sees Black churches and Black organizational structures within the church not as signs of segregation or separatism but as providing people the opportunity to choose. He wants his congregation to welcome Whites and presumes that white churches would welcome him. As he says, "I'm not discriminating when I have a church full of Black people." For Johnson, it's wrong for a congregation to tell people where they can or cannot worship, but it's not wrong to provide choices, some of which people make on the basis of culture and race.

It has been in the rapidly changing, evolving, confusing, and sometimes contradictory culture of the United States and Canada that the church growth movement surfaced in the 1960s as an attempt to find effective ways to evangelize. Led by Donald McGavran and Peter Wagner, with a training center at Fuller Theological Seminary in Pasadena, California, the church growth movement developed a strategy based on the homogeneous unit principle, which, according to some, is one of if not the most important key church growth principle. The homogeneous unit principle is built on an observation made by missiologist

Donald McGavran: "Men like to become Christians without crossing racial, linguistic, or class barriers."[6] That observation, made from missionary experiences in Papua New Guinea, was elaborated on and applied to the American experience by Peter Wagner in *Our Kind of People: The Ethical Dimensions of Church Growth in America,* in which he states, "I hope to argue convincingly that ethical justification for homogeneous churches exists in social-psychological, theological, and biblical sources."[7]

This defense of and support for culturally distinct congregations surfaced within the Evangelical church during and immediately following the civil rights era, when American society was for the first time facing the need to turn away from a history of white supremacy and segregation. For some the homogeneous unit sounded too much like a new name for the same old racism and separatism that has been American Christianity's as well as America's besetting sin. It appeared as a way to keep minorities out of predominately white churches.

In the early 1970s, I attended a seminar during which the homogeneous unit principle was being explained with a medical analogy. Church "diseases" were diagnosed and remedies prescribed to grow healthy congregations. We were told that one of the diseases that could prove fatal to a congregation was to be caught in a "changing neighborhood," a euphemism for an influx of racial minorities into a previously all-white neighborhood. I happened to be sitting beside a Nazarene pastor from our district, an immigrant from Guyana of African descent. Following the presentation, he said, "If this is true, then I represent a plague if I move into your neighborhood and attend your church."

In *Our Kind of People,* Wagner acknowledged that the homogeneous unit principle was controversial. In the view of Bill M. Sullivan, director of the Church Growth Division of the Church of the Nazarene, the idea of the homogeneous unit was unfortunately misplaced in the American

THE CHANGING FACE OF THE CHURCH

context and should never have become a central theme of the church growth movement. Sullivan received his doctor of ministry degree with a church growth emphasis from Fuller in 1985. He is the past president (1992) of the American Society of Church Growth and in 1993 received the society's Donald McGavran Award.

Sullivan said, "I tend to disagree with those who say that the homogeneous unit principle is fundamental to the church growth movement. I know there are still some who say that, and I disagree. The fundamental concern of the church growth movement, which was the founding burden of Donald McGavran, was 'Why is it that in our mission work in America we are not reaching out, not getting people saved, and over there in other world areas many people are getting saved and coming to Christ? Why is that, and could we possibly change our situation?'"

In a *Grow* magazine article, Sullivan wrote that "there is only one church growth principle."[8] In reference to the article, he said, "That principle is, what is the most effective way—that is ethical, that is biblical—of doing evangelism?" Concerning the origins of the homogeneous unit principle, he said:

At first promoting cultural separatism as a means of evangelism seemed the right thing. You have to remember back in those days there was this talk about Black is beautiful, and red is beautiful, and yellow and brown are beautiful. There was an affirmation of cultures. The homogeneous unit principle was not intended to be racist. It was intended to affirm the legitimacy of all those groups and to simply get evangelism in line. Even McGavran himself was highly supportive of the Civil Rights Movement. It was just an unfortunate thing that the homogeneous unit principle became so divisive. That's why most of the people I know have moved away from it because it is not right for our society. That is not an effective way to do evangelism.

As the face of America and the face of the churches change, Sullivan says that the church growth emphasis must adapt: "We need to work on the idea of inclusivity, of ultimately not having any kind of structures that tend to separate, but only those that tend to include. Everybody recognizes cultural variety, and we're trying to see how we can bring people together. That's why I like the idea of inclusivity—to work with these groups in order to create an inclusive, not a separatist, church."

Even though support for the homogeneous unit principle is in the past, the underlying issue remains. In the struggle over segregation and integration, the language of the Civil Rights Movement has given way to a new debate about multiculturalism, sometimes described as "cultural particularism." While multiculturalism correctly identifies the various cultures and subcultures in pluralistic American society, it tends toward ethnocentrism, a claim of cultural superiority.

This ethnocentric understanding of multiculturalism has become particularly divisive at secular and state universities. While multicultural studies teach the value and contribution of various cultures, multiculturalism, as an ism, has balkanized university communities, separating students both in classrooms and campus housing into hostile, exclusive subgroups.

As we look back in the light of the more recent trends, separatism and self-segregation in American society, it appears now that the homogeneous unit principle was simply stating the obvious. That is, people tend to congregate around common interests. The common denominator for a congregation may be language, race, class, or even worship and music. A culturally diverse congregation is a homogeneous unit in its own way, with its commitment to diversity being the glue that holds the people together.

Therefore, it may be better to recognize that every congregation has its own unique culture and is by definition a homogeneous unit. A group of people of whatever race, language, or neighborhood is not necessarily wrong nor, for that matter, right for wanting to worship together.

Multiculturalism recognizes and values cultural distinctiveness. White society is challenged to recognize that it continues to be influenced if not controlled by Eurocentrism, a view that contends that Western culture is the standard by which all others are to be judged. In reaction, Afrocentrism asserts that the origin, indeed the higher standard for culture and civilization, is found in the African heritage. On and on it goes in the cultural or multicultural wars.

The question from a biblical perspective in a pluralistic society is not the particular makeup of a congregation, but rather, does the congregation's distinctiveness include or exclude people who are different? The critical test is whether congregations, of whatever description, are inclusive or exclusive.

Inclusiveness is an undebatable gospel mandate. While Christian communities reflect a wide variety of cultural differences, if they are true to the gospel message they must include, not exclude, people regardless of individual and social differences. The inclusive gospel can hardly be proclaimed from an exclusive church.

Language differences are the most obvious and acceptable reason for culturally distinctive congregations. However, even the need to hear the gospel in an understandable language can lead to nativism, separatism, and exclusive faith communities. Most of us have been around bilingual people for whom English is a second language. It is not unusual for those who speak two languages to switch from English to another language if they want to exclude their English-only listeners from hearing the conversations. It's much easier than whispering or going off alone. When this happens, language serves as a barrier rather than a bridge to communication.

One may question the motivation of a group of people in the United States and English-speaking Canada, most of whom are conversant in English, who choose nevertheless to worship in a foreign language. If it is to reach first-generation immigrants, then obviously the language is a bridge. However, as many second-generation immigrant communities are finding, maintaining the language may become a barrier not only with the majority group but often with their own children. A Spanish, Asian, or even English-speaking congregation may be either exclusive or inclusive. Language can be used either as a bridge or a barrier in spreading the gospel and building up the household of faith.

Inclusiveness is more than a willingness, it is in fact a desire to recognize and celebrate diversity. Johnny Nells encourages the acceptance of Native Americans for the benefit of the majority community. He said, "An inclusive faith community will find ways to translate and communicate across language barriers." In the United States this might mean not only helping everyone to become fluent in the English language but also learning from minority language groups about how their cultures, as expressed in language, enrich the gospel message. It means that English-speaking congregations will be as willing to listen to sermons in another language through an interpreter as minority groups are commonly expected to do.

Racial divisions have been the scandal of American Christianity. The first African slaves were prevented from being evangelized. When converts began to appear, they were forbidden to participate in white congregations. It was rather late in colonial America before Africans who had become Americans were allowed to conduct their own worship services.

Segregated congregations were the result of philosophies of white supremacy and exclusion. The tradition of African-American Christianity was a necessary reaction to racism. Before and after the Civil War, the Black church was the only place where African-Americans could enjoy a limited degree of freedom with their own leadership. While race relations have improved, the same underlying attitudes that created the need for segregated congregations too often prevail. Exclusively white society and white congregations have remained separate because of aversion to people of African-American descent. Black people in America have responded by creating their own separate congregations, reacting to the rejection of the majority white community.

This historical context explains the very different reasons for the evolution of segregated churches. White congregations often excluded Nonwhites. Black congregations were organized to include the excluded, even Whites if they chose to attend.

Given the tragic history and legacy of American racism, it is no wonder that most white and Black people choose to worship with people like themselves. Few people will risk the rejection that often follows crossing over. Racial barriers may be more difficult to bridge than language differences.

The same biblical mandate applies to the majority and minority communities alike. While there are understandable historical explanations for separate congregations, any congregation, white or Black, compromises the biblical mandate when it excludes people simply because they are different.

It may be, however, a division in the church other than exclusiveness based on racial or language differences that more often than not violates the gospel message. In the New Testament, James condemns an early Christian community for excluding the poor. When poor people were not welcomed as warmly as the rich folks, he asked, "Have you not discriminated among yourselves and become judges with evil thoughts?" (2:4). The Scripture continues to condemn any kind of exclusion—in especially strong language: "If you show favoritism, you sin and are convicted by the law as lawbreakers" (v. 9).

In any language, and among all races, congregations often reflect the economic stratification that divides society between the rich and the poor. Yet even in this instance, economically segregated congregations may be either inclusive or exclusive. A congregation made up of prosperous people may nevertheless be inclusive if it recognizes the responsibility of stewardship and uses its financial resources to build the Kingdom by sharing with its poorer brothers and sisters and by seeking to change the conditions that condemn people to want and destitution. While it is unlikely that a congregation among economically disadvantaged people would tend to be exclusive, even the less well-off can become judgmental of those who happen to have more.

In the marketplace, where discrimination is now illegal, corporations have found it in their own economic self-interest to manage diversity well in order to become and remain profitable. Employees from the top down are being sensitized to cultural differences and instructed in how to take advantage of diversity. In some corporations this is important enough to have personnel permanently available to lead and train a workplace that reflects the pluralism of society.

Multiculturalism, notwithstanding its contribution to understanding the values of distinct cultures, as an ideology tends to divide and exclude, while the programs to manage cultural diversity seek to be certain that everyone is included. Diversity awareness and training stress the importance of a society and culture to which we all belong. Recognizing the potential divisiveness of cultural particularism, it encourages new social groupings. People from diverse groups learn to share things in common that unite rather than divide.

The challenge for multicultural ministries in the Church of the Nazarene is to unite rather than divide the church into increasing numbers of disconnected subgroups. The church could win the battle and lose the war if it is successful in promoting the growth of separate groups (that is, strategy committees, culturally distinct congregations, and organizational structures) without creating an inclusive church in which people are wanted, needed, and included regardless of their cultural, racial, or language identity. The challenge is not simply to be effective in expanding multicultural ministries but to build a multicultural church. The church has an opportunity to take advantage of diversity in extending the gospel in a fractured and frayed society. Minorities want something more than to be noticed. While they will resist assimilation if that means the discrediting of their culture, they do want and need to be included. The majority white community must adjust to the realities of a society in which minorities will soon become the majority. Exclusion and separatism will become, if not already so, as unproductive as they are wrong. The growth of the church, as well as profitability in the marketplace, will in the future depend upon being certain that everyone is included in the task of remaking the church as well as remaking America.

Dallas Mucci, district superintendent of the Metro New York District, described in the winter 1993-94 issue of *Grow* magazine how significant church growth has occurred in multicultural New York City.[9] While noting that the language minority congregations have been successful, he pointed out that most of the New York congregations include people from a variety of cultural backgrounds. In the interview he said, "While there are certain cultural enclaves, growth in our churches is sometimes quickened because of cultural affinity; but overall, New York is a world-class city with less racial tension than most of the cities of the world. Thus, many of our faster-growing churches are multicultural in makeup, just like the city." Mucci observed that while congregations often begin around some narrow cultural or language identity, they remain open to people of various cultural backdrops and participate in a regional denominational fellowship, which includes and unites a wide variety of people in shared leadership as well as cooperative worship. Diversity within the churches has become an advantage.

Not all cities and communities are as congenial to cross-cultural contact as Mucci claims for New York City. Inclusiveness may not be welcomed in neighborhoods defined by the barriers that divide people from one another. Mucci expresses his conviction that the inclusive fellowship enjoyed by Nazarenes at Metro New York District gatherings is a sign of the Kingdom: "Our district assembly and its celebration raise hopes for mutual love and trust in the church for all people."

5

Diversity Leadership

Leadership Style and Issues for the 21st Century

*D*IVERSITY LEADERSHIP HAS BECOME AN ESSENTIAL CONCERN of American business and industry. The bottom line of profitability has led the economic sector to understand the "diversity advantage." On the negative side, workplace discrimination against minorities and women results in costly legal battles. Companies have discovered that they can be more profitable with leaders who are good at managing diversity. They have also learned that a diverse management and sales organization leads to greater profitability in domestic markets as well as expanding foreign economies.

The church, too, has a bottom line. While the church growth movement is about more than numbers and building large churches, it is about growing the church. It is about growing healthy churches passionate about going everywhere proclaiming the Good News and faithful to the great commandment to love God and neighbor unconditionally. Those in the church who react to the suggestion of learning from business may be reminded of Jesus' teaching in which He told the disciples, "The sons of this world are more shrewd in dealing with their own generation than

71

the sons of light" (Luke 16:8, RSV). It may still be true that the most segregated hour of the week is 11:00 Sunday morning. What the Civil Rights Movement seemed unable to do—to cause Black and white Americans to need and want, if not like, one another—it may be that business has begun to accomplish. It makes good business sense to have a workplace in which people are accepted for what they can contribute. Furthermore, it is a good investment to train workers and leaders alike in how to be aware of and more sensitive to cultural diversity.

To achieve its bottom-line mission objectives, the church, too, will need to embrace diversity as an advantage rather than see it as an obstacle. Congregations can no longer run from changing neighborhoods. All neighborhoods are changing. To successfully carry through with the mandate to "make disciples of all nations" (Matt. 28:19)—the English word "nations" could more accurately be translated "ethnics"—will require new strategies and leaders who are prepared to guide the church through changes needed to remain faithful to, as well as be successful in, its mission. A description of the leader of the future and some of the issues facing the church follow in this chapter.

Maria L. Johnson is a vice president responsible for the Office of Diversity at the Federal National Mortgage Association (FNMA, or Fannie Mae) headquarters in Washington, D.C. Trained in law, she has a full-time staff of more than a dozen people working with the 3,000 on-site employees at America's largest investor in home mortgages. Her responsibility is not only to arbitrate disputes when necessary but, more important, to train employees, especially those in management, about the importance of treating everyone fairly.

In a city with a majority of minorities, Fannie Mae has a good record of hiring women and minorities. When I asked about her mission, she said, "I'm not here to save souls, just to help us make money. We can't be profitable if people are suing one another and involving the company in legal battles. I just want to be sure everyone is treated fairly." She went on to say that not every claim of discrimination is warranted; in fact, only about 25 percent of the challenges are decided in favor of the complainant. But a complaint usually is symptomatic of poor management, she said. Under the direction of Fannie Mae's Board of Directors and the chief executive officer, she has developed training materials for every level of the organization, providing constant monitoring of how well the company is doing at being inclusive in order to be profitable.

It will take equal determination and intention for the church to be faithful to and successful in its mission. If corporations with financial interests as their primary concern but with no moral (let alone biblical) mandate see the need for inclusion, how much more should the church engage in the task of monitoring itself and providing the management and leadership skills needed for the future.

John W. Work, a management and leadership training specialist, has written several books and training manuals for major corporations. In his book *What Every CEO Already Knows About Managing Diversity*,[1] he calls on American business leaders to include in their skills the capacity to work with and nurture minorities in order to keep pace with rapid changes in the workplace. I first met Dr. Work in Washington, D.C., in 1988 when he was providing consultative services to the American Red Cross headquarters during the time when Nazarene layman Richard Schubert was the American Red Cross president and CEO. It was there that he furthered his interests in helping the nonprofit world as well as religious communities develop diversity management and leadership strategies.

It is not enough for organizations to declare their openness to minorities and women. The culture of the organization must change. "Infusion" describes the result in an organization into which minorities are brought without taking advantage of their unique interests and contribution. This is sometimes referred to as assimilation. The burden of responsibility has been on the minorities to make all the changes. "Inclusion" describes the process in an organization in which leaders welcome minorities and assume responsibility for making changes in the culture of the organization. This intention is expressed in the brochure mentioned earlier titled *Diversity Leadership in the Church of the Nazarene:*

> We view diversity and inclusiveness as both a critical theological issue and a moral imperative. In today's changing world, the success of our mission depends upon attracting committed and dedicated people as parishioners and as leaders of our widely spread denomination.
>
> It also depends upon innovation, wisdom, and sophisticated insight. Thus the Church of the Nazarene needs people who come from different backgrounds and bring fresh approaches and unique ideas for the carrying out of our mission.
>
> Using the gifts and talents of multitudes of people with differing perspectives and experiences requires encouraging and supporting their growth and input, integrating them wholly into our teams, and deepening our understanding of how to work, pray, and live together.
>
> If we in the Church of the Nazarene are to achieve our mission, we must learn to seek, value, and relish diversity to make it a basis for strength, not a hurdle to overcome.

The saying goes that managers are charged with "doing things right," while leaders have responsibility for "doing the right thing." In his article "Leading a Diverse Work Force" in the 1996 Drucker Foundation publication *The Leader of the Future,* John Work challenges leaders to step forward and accept responsibility for articulating the values that benefit society as a whole. In Work's opinion, a leader must be more than the manager of an organization. Leadership "requires individuals to take considerable risks and to do things that others are not willing to do." He writes, "True leaders will recognize the opportunities and potential benefits inherent in diversity. . . . In the final analysis, true leadership brings people of diverse backgrounds and interest together in ways that provide fair and equitable opportunities to contribute their best, achieve personal goals, and realize their full potential."[2]

The diversity leadership issues facing the church are no less challenging than for any other segment of society. The issues are constantly changing. There are no pat answers. There is no "one size fits all" multicultural program for the church to adopt. The historic and immigrant minority groups are all different. Hispanics are often incorrectly lumped into a single category when in fact the Hispanic world contains its own diversity with people of native, African, and European descent from more than 20 countries. The same is true of Portuguese-speaking people from Brazil (South America's largest country by land and population), the Cape Verde Islands, and Mozambique. Even the English-speaking white majority is hardly homogeneous. The Appalachian Strategy Committee was formed in 1993 to develop regional plans to more effectively reach a predominately white segment of the American population whom those on the committee would describe as culturally distinct.

What is possible and necessary from leaders is an awareness of and appreciation for the wide variety of cultures within the church family in America and worldwide. The church needs leaders who can see beyond their own cultural boundaries, leaders who can help create a new community. Leaders of the 21st-century church—local pastors with their lay leaders, district and general leaders together—will be called upon to address the following issues:

- Cross-cultural ministry skills
- Organizational changes for an inclusive church

- Neighborhood-based congregations
- The United States as a mission field
- Women in ministry
- Preserving properties in key urban areas

Cross-cultural Ministry Skills

Diversity training materials attempt to help leaders understand that very often cultural conflicts are conflicts of style rather than of substance. Well-intentioned people from different cultural perspectives will sometimes clash, not because they differ in motive and mission, but because they communicate differently and will follow different means to achieve the same end. This is not to reduce all disagreement or truth, for that matter, to perspective. It is to recognize that unless leaders deal constructively with conflicts that result from differing cultural perspectives, it is almost impossible to achieve genuine agreement. Kent Hill, president of Eastern Nazarene College, likes to quote G. K. Chesterton to the effect that "genuine disagreement is very difficult to achieve." Much of the time our disagreements are misunderstandings born of poor communication.

Leadership training for ministry in the United States and Canada may be as strenuous as the cross-cultural and language training expected of missionaries sent to countries made up of one dominant culture and language (such as Haiti, Swaziland, Guatemala). United States cities are polycultural. Educators in Chicago and Los Angeles, for instance, report that their school districts include children from 100 or more different home languages. Many Nazarene districts now have congregations worshiping and conducting their business in several different languages. The church leader of the future will have to manage ministries among several different language and racial groups in one district assembly, youth camp, or congregation. At the 1994 Multicultural Ministries Conference in Nashville, Mike Estep told the delegates that in the future every Nazarene minister to some degree will have to be multicultural, as was the apostle Paul.[3]

No one can be expected to learn all the languages or understand everything about all the cultures, but leaders can be expected to make a place in the leadership ranks and the rooms where decisions are made for appropriate representation for every perspective within the church family. Learning how to create unity from all this diversity is the challenge for the leader of tomorrow.

The Multicultural Ministries challenge for church leadership is to bring people together, even in congregations. In a place like New York it is a decided advantage to have a good mix of languages and cultures in every congregation. As Metro New York District Superintendent Dallas Mucci says, "When you go into a place like Flushing, what you want in your church is English-speaking people, you want Asians, you want Latins, you want White, you want Black, you want island Blacks, you want Filipinos. You hope you can have all those. That gives you a real chance, because Flushing is the most integrated neighborhood in the city, where the people have lived together now for a number of years with minimal racial strife." He went on to say that diversity gives a congregation vision for all the different people moving into a neighborhood. "They will reach out to them. They won't run from them. They're not afraid of them. They see them as people to be evangelized. They see Flushing as a mission field. That to me is a great advantage. It never threatens the church."

Leaders will be called upon to see that diversity both inside and outside the church is recognized as an advantage, an opportunity for the church to achieve its fundamental mission.

Organizational Changes for an Inclusive Church

One of the biggest challenges for present church leaders, most of whom are white males, is to make room for and provide the organizational structures that intentionally bring minorities and women into visible leadership responsibilities. This is not to call for a denominational version of affirmative action, but rather a strategic decision. While there is a moral and spiritual overtone to the call for representative, inclusive organizational structures, the church needs to make the changes in order to be more effective in achieving its bottom line, that is, being faithful to and successful in its mission to grow the church.

Relying upon the democracy that governs most of the elected processes in the Church of the Nazarene may not be serving the church well. Robert Scott, director of the Hiram F. Reynolds Research Institute, which is charged with providing strategic planning advice to the Board of General Superintendents, said, "We have to admit that democracy is flawed. Democracy is not the answer." The institute has identified denominational "core competencies," one of which is the Nazarene commitment to be an international fellowship. Scott says, "We want to see ourselves as this international global family that crosses national lines, connected by mission, working with an inclusive spirit through local congregations and communities of faith." On the subject of leadership he goes on to say that "the only way we can be a viable international church is to be a church with multicultural leadership."

"I don't think we can depend on the democratic process to produce Kingdom results," says Jesse Middendorf, pastor of Kansas City First Church of the Nazarene. "I think we need to take some intentional steps to create opportunity for leadership to be placed rather than to allow it merely to surface. In our national history, in our denominational history, we have not recognized the need to cultivate leadership among minorities."

Middendorf and others are calling for intentional changes in our leadership selection processes. Jerry Porter, superintendent of the Washington District, says, "We have to conscientiously promote minority leaders into visible positions of leadership. In the nominating and election process, women and minority leaders will most often not be elected. They are going to have to be appointed. And so, we need at-large membership on boards and a few positions that can be filled by appointment to help us get minorities represented."

Paragraph 330.1 of the *Manual of the Church of the Nazarene* hints at the need for diverse representation on the General Board with this instruction to district nominating committees: "The multicultural composition of the nominating district should be considered in selecting names for nomination."[4] However, there were no minorities elected from the United States and Canada at the 1993 General Assembly. The only woman on the General Board from the United States was the ex officio president of the Nazarene World Mission Society.

Porter sees the Multicultural Ministries office and the multicultural strategy committees as being steps in the right direction: "One of the most obvious changes is the strategy committees. I think that's been very necessary. We don't have to apologize for a strategy group to reach a target group. We don't have to feel that somehow these strategy groups are segregating the church. I think they are helping us be culturally sensitive to the target we're trying to reach. And we'll never reach people for Christ unless we do it in the context of a message that they understand within their culture."

Church structures are always a means to an end, subject to change, and in need of constant review and evaluation. The shape of the church must be determined by its mission.

Neighborhood-Based Congregations

Even though churches are commonly identified by and identify with the neighborhoods or cities in which they are located, many if not most Nazarene churches are not neighborhood based. Congregations both large and small are typically supported and attended by commuting members. In large metropolitan areas, people have tended to choose churches as they might select a restaurant. It's been said that people will drive a long way for either a good meal or a good sermon.

Jesse Middendorf points out that the Church of the Nazarene is a denomination of small churches. "Typically the small church becomes a sociological network or unit in which like attracts like. Relationships create the boundaries within which the church tends to function. It may have started with an attempt to reach the community. The reality is that over a relatively brief period of time the majority of those churches move out of a community focus and become relationally focused. It is my experience, my observation with some empirical evidence, that we predominately are relationally structured rather than geographically structured."

The leadership challenge, especially for pastors, is to guide congregations through the changes needed in order for a congregation to become neighborhood based while retaining its family or relational qualities of life so important for faith communities. Speaking for Kansas City First Church, Middendorf says, "We want to be an influence in this community." Among other things, the church has become a meeting place for neighborhood associations and a polling place for major elections. He thinks of this as "pre-evangelism." Neighbors who see the church as a neighborhood-based congregation are beginning to respond. "What began as a trickle has become an interesting tide. It's not a flood yet, but it's an interesting tide. Nearly every week a new family from the neighborhood is coming."

Pastors like Middendorf will continue to struggle with changing neighborhoods and the changing boundaries of faith communities. He asks, "How do we maintain the sense of continuity and community while we're reaching across all kinds of boundaries and barriers? As I see Jesus in the New Testament confronting Judaism as He did, that was part of the issue He was dealing with. How far are we willing to reach out across the boundaries? Can we reach from Jerusalem to Judea? Can we reach from Judea to Samaria? Can we do that socially, culturally, geographically? I think the church is always going to be caught in that tension, and reaching across is intentional. We don't do it accidentally."

The United States as a Mission Field

In his address to the 1994 Multicultural Ministries Conference,[5] Paul Cunningham made a strong appeal to recognize the fact that the cities of America have become mission fields. While the challenge of missions has motivated the church to extend itself to more than 100 world areas, with growth everywhere missionaries have been sent, the mission fields close to home have yet to attract the same attention and response. The church has proven that with dedicated, trained missionaries almost any target population will respond. The recent growth of minorities within the church in the past decade is largely the by-product of successful missionary work in the home countries of the immigrant Nazarenes rather than any missionary planning to reach minority people in the United States.

Home missions have been replaced by the idea of church planting. "Church planters" for the most part have been bivocational, entrepreneurial pastors who are willing to try starting churches with a few people and minimal resources. As would be expected in a denomination that is near 90 percent English-speaking white, most church planting goes on with the majority community, with very little of the church planting people and resources directed to minority populations.

The leadership challenge is to develop the missionary

strategies for the United States and Canada like those that have proven successful wherever they have been employed worldwide. Church leaders will need to act upon the realization that the United States and Canada are mission fields by creating the organizational structures needed to make good use of missionaries and the financial resources needed to sustain a serious missionary enterprise. Robert Scott says, "One of the things I feel very strongly about personally is that the mission field of the Church of the Nazarene has to include officially the United States and Canada. I don't know all the mechanics by which it would eventually be accomplished, but I believe it represents an urgent step in the whole incarnational ministry of the church and the maturational ministry of the church, especially in this thing of becoming a multicultural church."

To train, appoint, and support missionaries in the United States and Canada will require a change in definition as well as organizational structure. Traditional missiologists have defined missionaries as those who cross cultural and national boundaries. The popular image has been a full-time career missionary who learns a language and spends a lifetime in a remote area of the world untouched by the gospel message. All of this is changing.

A far-reaching development occurred during the 1995 meeting of the General Board of the Church of the Nazarene. It was during this time that the denomination expanded its definition of a missionary. Historically, the church's commitment in world mission has been through a career missionary path. Lifelong terms of service were the norm. Since the world and its boundaries and cultures have changed so much during the past 25 years, the missionary effort is being expanded to include and recognize short-term missionary assignments. These include Nazarenes In Volunteer Service (NIVS) as well as the many people who pay their own way for special tasks that need to be performed. This is the best way for the Church of the

Nazarene to reach its goal of 1,000 missionaries as the term is redefined. While the approach may change, the end result is still the same: reaching the lost for Christ.

In its 100-year history, the church has thrived, in part, because of its missionary commitment to be a sending church, sending its money with its sons and daughters wherever there is need and opportunity to spread the gospel. The church is being called to new global mission, a missionary strategy that reaches out to people close by as well as far off. As a result of immigration and inevitable global population changes, the cities of the United States and Canada have become as foreign as any so-called foreign country to the English-speaking white people who make up 90 percent of the members of the Church of the Nazarene in these countries. It is no exaggeration to describe these urban areas as "mission fields."

Missionary opportunities are present everywhere in the United States and Canada. Missionary candidates—full-time career, volunteers, and tentmakers—are ready to serve. The challenge for church leaders is to adjust the "mechanics," as Dr. Scott put it, so that the shape of the church is determined by its mission.

Women in Ministry

There are Nazarenes around who remember a generation or two ago when a significant number of evangelists and pastors in the Church of the Nazarene were women.[6] According to Nina Gunter, Nazarene World Mission Society executive director, women are again preparing for ministry and are ready to serve if given the opportunity: "I would say that the potential for gain is very strong. I understand that 20 percent of the enrollment at Nazarene Theological Seminary in Kansas City are women."

However, according to Gunter, it has never been more difficult for women to find their place in male-dominated pastoral and leadership positions: "As far as women placed in ministry, I understand that we are about as low as we've ever been. And to think that in 1930, 30 percent of Nazarene ministers were women. What concerns me is that we have outstanding potential Nazarene women ministers who are leaving the denomination. In December I had two calls in one week. One was a fourth-generation Nazarene who said, 'Nina, I've got to leave. My church has no place for me.' Sad. Nazarene women ministers are going to the Presbyterians, Lutherans, and Methodists, who are taking them because our women have fire in their souls."

The important contribution that women leaders are making in other segments of society and within other denominations is lacking in the Church of the Nazarene. As we move from being a male-dominated society to a female and multicultural one, the church, like other institutions, faces a major challenge. Today, women hold important positions in business, education, and other types of organizations. They supervise large staffs. They are responsible for sizable budgets. Yet, when it comes to work and positions in a local congregation, their roles are often very confined. Lay development should encourage and support women, not only in ministry but in leadership and governance as well; not for gender's sake alone but because the female talent is available and untapped.

The same democratic structures that work against minorities are not serving the church well in its need and opportunity to include women in ministry. Dr. Gunter suggests that diversity leadership training should encourage congregations and district superintendents to consider women as pastors. "One of the best steps," she said, "would be for a woman to become a district superintendent in the United States. There is a woman district superintendent and three women college presidents outside the United States."

This recent decline of women ministers results to some degree, according to Gunter, from the influence of theological Fundamentalism—"because in our church some of the models for our preachers and congregations are people who are Fundamentalists in theology, which means they do not believe in a woman being in the pulpit or a woman being a leader." She added, "Their theology is affecting our church in a stronger way than we admit." When asked about the men-only Promise Keepers movement, she said, "Well, personally I don't have any problem with that. There are conferences for men. There are conferences for women. The only question or request I would make is—in excluding women—that they recognize that women are called of God to be preachers." She would prefer that the clergy conferences convened by Promise Keepers make it clear that it is for "men pastors," not just "pastors," which tends to support the notion that pastors are, or perhaps even should be, men.

If the face of the church is to look anything like America, women must be prominent in the pulpit as well as in the pew. The 1993 General Assembly passed this brief resolution concerning the place of women in ministry: "We support the right of women to use their God-given spiritual gifts within the church. We affirm the historic right of women to be elected and appointed to places of leadership within the Church of the Nazarene."[7] It remains for rank-and-file members as well as leaders to follow through with good intentions.

Preserving Properties in Key Urban Areas

The success of ministries among minorities will hinge to some degree upon finding available properties, particularly in urban areas. Regrettably, church buildings in strategic areas have been sold by relocating congregations, leaving congregations and districts with almost insurmountable financial burdens as they try to reenter these areas of opportunity.

Dallas Mucci of the Metro New York District says,

"The Church of the Nazarene, which had in effect started in the cities, gave away those properties—didn't actually give them away, but sold those properties off at a low price in areas that could be prime for us." He cited some examples. "In Yonkers we had a church that we sold for $20,000—a very nice building. The church that bought it is outgrowing it. We tried to purchase it back, and the cost was $420,000. We couldn't plant a church at that beginning cost. Interestingly, in another area where we had a strong church, right where our district office and parsonage now are located—in Mount Vernon—the church in Mount Vernon was sold for a very small amount of money, and now we are having to rent property to establish our first Portuguese-speaking church. It is costing us $1,400 a month to plant a church where we still would have had a church if we had not given away the building at such a low price."

In his message to the Multicultural Ministries Conference in Nashville, General Superintendent Paul Cunningham called for a partnership of local, district, and general church interests to provide a means to retain properties even when congregations relocate. In some instances, local congregations and districts have taken the initiative to be sure that, if at all possible, buildings remain as a resource or, if buildings are sold, that some of the proceeds are used to secure adequate facilities for beginning a new church in the same area. Since local congregations need the approval of the district to buy and sell properties, this is one area where general and district leaders can work with local congregations to be sure that property decisions are made with strategic mission goals and objectives in mind.

A rather recent creative use of properties to reach language minority groups has been the shared-space ministries, often referred to as "multicongregational ministries." There are many variations on this theme. At Los Angeles First Church, four congregations have formed a federation with equal access to and responsibility for the property. More typically, a host congregation, usually English-speaking white, invites a language minority group to worship in its building temporarily. The Multicultural Ministries office has prepared a handbook on multicongregational ministries with dos and don'ts and examples. More than 100 buildings are being used in this way.[8]

While a few of the shared-spaced ministries may be permanent, for most congregations it's a temporary arrangement at best, and unless entered into with much forethought and flexibility, it can be the cause of misunderstanding. Dale Jones, director of the Church Growth Research office, has observed that the Nazarene culture "assumes that if it's a real church, it's got to get its own building." However inconvenient, the need for property is so urgent that having more than one congregation in the few buildings available is the only way for some to get started.

All this adds urgency to the recommendation for denominational procedures that help make the right decisions regarding strategic properties, without which the vision of a church expanding among minorities will be frustrated.

Overriding all these specific issues, and others that will surely surface, is the need for church leaders in America who will apply the truth of the Wesleyan-Holiness tradition in transcultural language, who will hold up the shared values of an inclusive Nazarene community in which all members contribute to the development of the church. Only with such leadership in local churches and denominational offices can the church find a way to bring new vision and passion to the 21st century.

6

Conclusion

A Church That Looks like the World

IF CURRENT GLOBAL CHURCH OF THE NAZARENE GROWTH PAT-terns continue, the 1997 General Assembly in San Antonio will be marked as the last in which the American delegation will be in the majority. In the first General Assembly after the turn of the century, in 2001, delegates representing world areas where Nazarene missions have flourished for nearly a century will outnumber American delegates.

Along with the increasing number of minorities in the United States and within the American church, the Church of the Nazarene in the 21st century will look much different than it has in the past. It will no longer be divided between a sending (American) church and a receiving (the rest of the world) church. Even though the American church for the foreseeable future will continue to provide most of the financial support for Nazarene ministries and missions, the church's resources and strategies in America and around the world will be directed by an international, multicultural leadership team.

It may be that some within the American church will begin to feel outnumbered at a General Assembly in which most of the delegates are from somewhere else, as they may feel threatened by the close proximity of a growing minority population within, as well as outside, the church. But if the American church remains true to its missionary vision, these changes will be seen as the answer to years of prayer, sacrificial giving, and dedicated mission work around the world. Persons privileged to attend the first General Assembly of the 21st century will see an international, multicultural church that looks more like the world than at any time in the past.

The American church will have the privilege of being a part of a larger inclusive global fellowship. The changing face of the church is beginning even now to resemble the vision of John the Revelator, who was inspired to see the gathered Church Triumphant "from every tribe and tongue and people and nation" (Rev. 5:9, RSV). As that vision in the Revelation of John followed the Church's struggle to be faithful to its mission, so the Church of the 21st century will sometimes be hard-pressed to maintain its unity and uniqueness in fractured and frayed societies.

At the turn of the 20th century a new hymn was written holding out the vision of a global Christian fellowship unifying believers around the world. The first verse reads:

In Christ there is no East or West,
In Him no South or North;
But one great fellowship of love
Throughout the whole wide earth.

—John Oxenham

As the 21st century nears, that's still the vision the Church follows. It's more than an organizational strategy. As the hymn writer above put it, Christian unity is rooted in Christ. The vision of an international, multicultural church is not simply in order to make Christ known. On the contrary, where Christ is known and followed, the church *is* an international, multicultural fellowship.

Appendix 1

**Statistical Charts on Growth Among
Nazarene Minorities in the United States and
Canada, from the Church Growth
Research Center**

Appendix 2

**Credentialed Ministers
by Gender and Role
in the Church of the Nazarene**

Appendix 3

Statement on Inclusive language

Appendix 1
MULTICULTURAL STATISTICS: CANADA AND U.S.A.

Group	1/1/70 Works	1/1/80 Works	1/1/90 Works	FOCs	2/7/97 CTMs	LBCs	Inac.	1995* Members	1995* SS Att.	1995* SS Enr.	1995* Raised
African-American	62	75	120	89	12	0	11	8,043	4,988	10,235	$ 2,788,248
Arab	0	0	10	6	1	1	1	271	198	318	60,893
Armenian	0	1	8	7	0	0	2	356	221	356	189,546
Cambodian	0	0	13	4	6	1	0	480	391	678	38,675
Chinese	5	5	18	14	4	3	0	917	521	838	593,701
Deaf/Hard of Hearing	0	0	1	1	0	0	1	13	0	0	0
Eritrean	0	0	2	4	2	0	1	37	144	211	43,053
Eskimo	1	1	1	1	0	0	0	30	17	118	30,333
Filipino	1	1	14	10	1	3	1	463	314	710	232,843
Finnish	0	0	1	0	0	0	0	0	0	0	0
Formosan	0	0	1	0	0	0	0	0	0	0	0
French	0	1	7	3	0	1	3	0	7	9	0
Haitian	0	4	43	53	10	1	2	6,152	4,241	5,985	896,091
Hispanic	68	105	225	195	68	12	28	11,058	10,719	21,753	4,978,447
Italian	0	0	1	1	0	0	0	28	0	0	120
Japanese	1	1	2	0	0	1	0	0	0	0	0
Jewish	0	0	1	1	0	0	1	0	0	0	0
Korean	0	14	54	45	11	2	8	3,117	1,623	2,906	1,604,538
Laotian	0	0	10	3	1	2	1	216	239	283	994
Micronesian	0	0	0	1	0	0	1	32	0	0	0
Multicultural**	1	1	26	106	5	2	5	15,260	8,524	19,888	12,821,836
Native American	32	42	56	43	11	3	3	2,016	1,452	2,801	492,926
Portuguese	2	3	4	4	2	1	0	304	361	512	219,067
Russian	0	0	0	1	0	1	0	0	60	250	0
Samoan	1	2	5	8	4	0	0	788	617	900	138,750
South Asian	0	1	6	6	0	0	0	236	140	198	45,618
Tamil	0	0	1	2	2	0	1	62	0	0	9,984
Vietnamese	0	0	5	3	0	0	0	277	182	157	64,812
West Indian	9	13	16	16	1	0	2	1,647	1,327	2,283	1,133,011
				(627	141	34	72)				
Totals	183	270	651			874		51,803	36,286	71,389	$26,383,486
				Active Total	802						

The 183 works for 1/1/70 include 180 FOCs and 3 CTMs.
The 270 works for 1/1/80 include 235 FOCs, 33 CTMs, and 2 LBCs.
The 651 works for 1/1/90 include 424 FOCs, 140 CTMs, 65 LBCs, and 22 inactive.
*Assembly minutes.
**Used here of congregations that are composed of several cultural groups, none of which predominate.

Updated from general secretary's records as of February 7, 1997.

NAZARENE GROWTH AMONG MULTICULTURAL GROUPS
United States, 1986-96

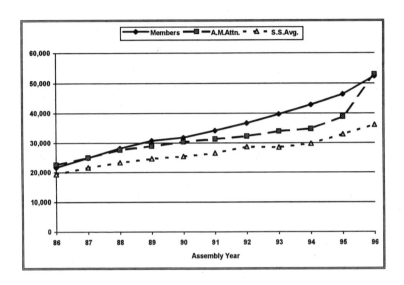

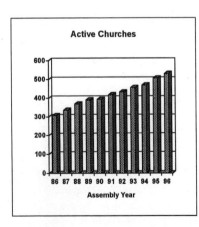

In 1996 there were 530 active Churches of the Nazarene that reported a primary cultural group other than White, English-speaking.

These churches reported a combined membership of 52,444; a total A.M. attendance of 43,102; and a Sunday School average of 36,218.

This is a net growth of 224 churches since 1986 and a membership increase of 142 percent over the same time period.

Prepared by the Church Growth Research Center from statistics reported annually to the general secretary, January 1997.

NAZARENE GROWTH AMONG AFRICAN-AMERICANS
in the United States, 1986-96

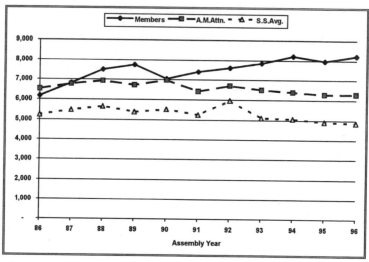

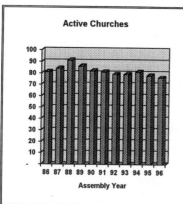

In 1996 there were 76 active Churches of the Nazarene that reported African-American as the primary cultural group.

African-American congregations reported a combined membership of 8,232; a total A.M. attendance of 6,299; and a Sunday School average of 4,868.

This is a net decline of 5 churches since 1986 and a 33.2 percent increase in members over the same time period. Many churches previously reported as African-American are now classified as multicultural.

Prepared by the Church Growth Research Center from statistics reported annually to the general secretary, January 1997.

Appendix 1

NAZARENE GROWTH AMONG ARABS
in the United States
1986-96

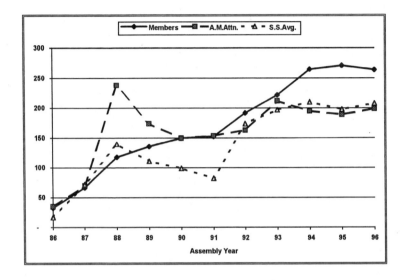

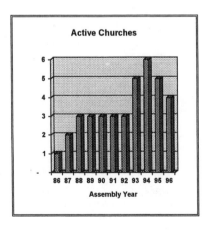

In 1996 there were 4 active Churches of the Nazarene that reported Arab as the primary cultural group.

Arab congregations reported a combined membership of 264; a total A.M. attendance of 199; and a Sunday School average of 208.

This is a net growth of 3 churches since 1986 and an increase in membership of 700 percent over the same time period.

Prepared by the Church Growth Research Center from statistics reported annually to the general secretary, January 1997.

95

NAZARENE GROWTH AMONG ARMENIANS
in the United States
1986-96

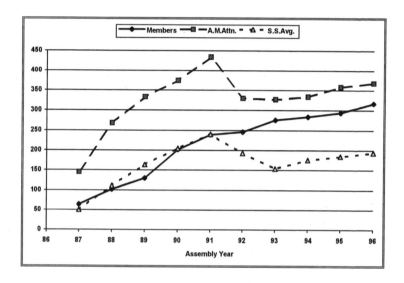

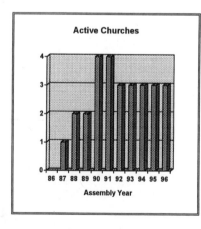

In 1996 there were 3 active Churches of the Nazarene that reported Armenian as the primary cultural group.

Armenian congregations reported a combined membership of 317; a total A.M. attendance of 368; and a Sunday School average of 194.

This is a net growth of 3 churches since 1986 and an increase of 317 members over the same time period.

Prepared by the Church Growth Research Center from statistics reported annually to the general secretary, January 1997.

NAZARENE GROWTH AMONG CAMBODIANS
in the United States
1986-96

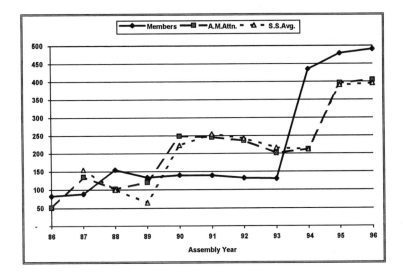

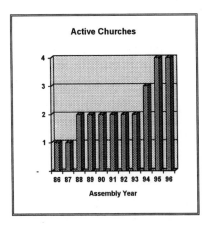

In 1996 there were 4 active Churches of the Nazarene that reported Cambodian as the primary cultural group.

Cambodian congregations reported a combined membership of 491; a total A.M. attendance of 405; and a Sunday School average of 396.

This is a net growth of 3 churches since 1986 and a membership increase of 492 percent over the same time period.

Prepared by the Church Growth Research Center from statistics reported annually to the general secretary, January 1997.

NAZARENE GROWTH AMONG CHINESE
in the United States
1986-96

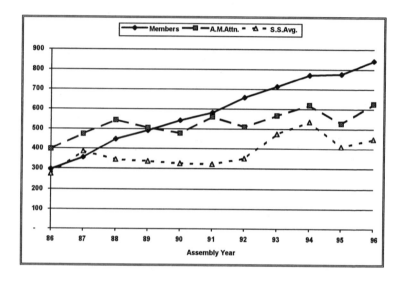

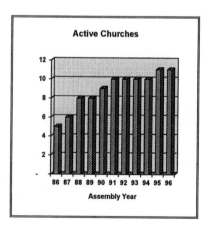

In 1996 there were 11 active Churches of the Nazarene that reported Chinese as the primary cultural group.

Chinese congregations reported a combined membership of 843; a total A.M. attendance of 626; and a Sunday School average of 449.

This is a net growth of 6 churches since 1986 and an increase of 185 percent in membership over the same time period.

Prepared by the Church Growth Research Center from statistics reported annually to the general secretary, January 1997.

NAZARENE GROWTH AMONG ERITREANS
in the United States
1986-96

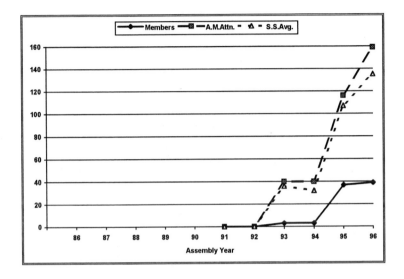

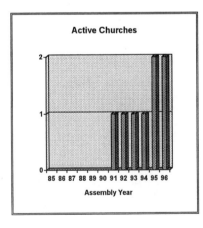

In 1996 there were 2 active Churches of the Nazarene that reported Eritrean as the primary cultural group.

These churches reported a full membership of 39; average A.M. attendance of 159; and a Sunday School average of 135.

This is a net growth of 2 churches since 1986 and an increase of 39 members over the same time period.

Prepared by the Church Growth Research Center from statistics reported annually to the general secretary, January 1997.

NAZARENE GROWTH AMONG FILIPINOS
in the United States
1986-96

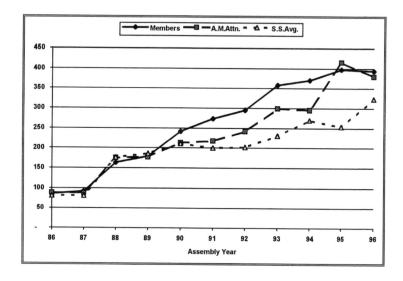

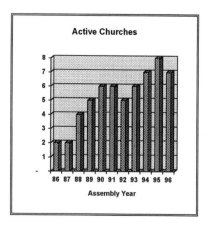

In 1996 there were 7 active Churches of the Nazarene that reported Filipino as the primary cultural group.

Filipino congregations reported a combined membership of 394; a total A.M. attendance of 380; and a Sunday School average of 323.

This is a net growth of 5 churches since 1986 and an increase of 358 percent in membership over the same time period.

Prepared by the Church Growth Research Center from statistics reported annually to the general secretary, January 1997.

NAZARENE GROWTH AMONG HAITIANS
in the United States
1986-96

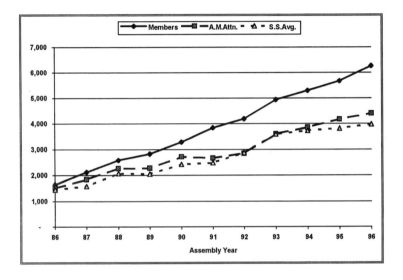

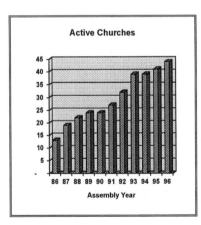

In 1996 there were 44 active Churches of the Nazarene that reported Haitian as the primary cultural group.

These churches reported a combined membership of 6,274; a total A.M. attendance of 4,402; and a Sunday School average of 3,981.

This is a net increase of 31 churches since 1986 and a 280 percent increase in members over the same time period.

Prepared by the Church Growth Research Center from statistics reported annually to the general secretary, January 1997.

NAZARENE GROWTH AMONG HISPANICS
in the United States
1986-96

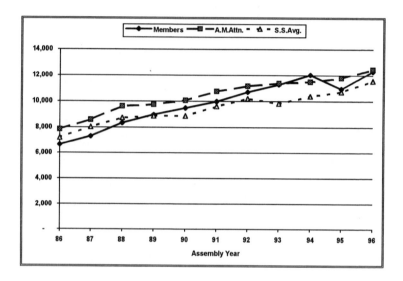

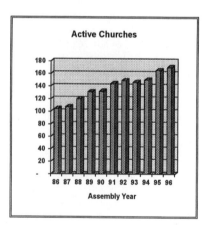

In 1996 there were 170 active Churches of the Nazarene that reported Hispanic as the primary cultural group.

These churches reported a combined membership of 12,316; a total A.M. attendance of 12,471; and a Sunday School average of 11,572.

This is a net growth of 66 churches since 1986 and an increase of 85 percent in membership over the same time period.

Prepared by the Church Growth Research Center from statistics reported annually to the general secretary, January 1997.

NAZARENE GROWTH AMONG JAPANESE
in the United States
1984-94

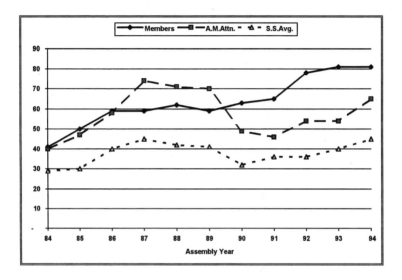

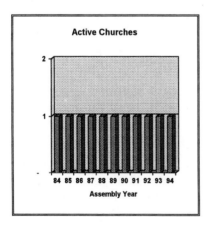

In 1994 there was 1 active Church of the Nazarene that reported Japanese as the primary cultural group.

This church reported a membership of 81; an A.M. attendance of 65; and a Sunday School average of 45.

This is the same number of churches as in 1984 and an increase of 98 percent in membership over the same time period.

Prepared by the Church Growth Research Center from statistics reported annually to the general secretary, May 1995.

NAZARENE GROWTH AMONG KOREANS
in the United States
1986-96

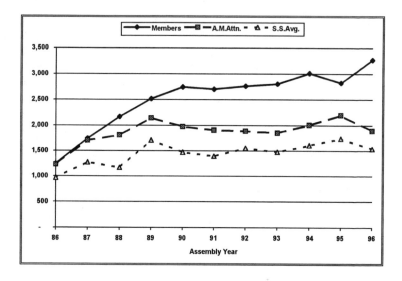

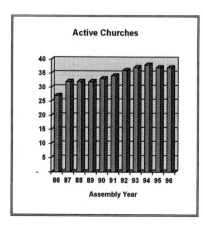

In 1996 there were 37 active Churches of the Nazarene that reported Korean as the primary cultural group.

These churches reported a combined membership of 3,272; a total A.M. attendance of 1,894; and a Sunday School average of 1,544.

This is a net growth of 10 churches since 1986 and an increase of 162 percent in membership over the same time period.

Prepared by the Church Growth Research Center from statistics reported annually to the general secretary, January 1997.

NAZARENE GROWTH AMONG LAOTIANS
in the United States
1986-96

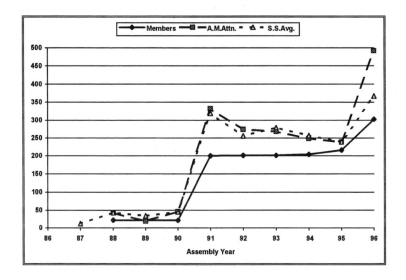

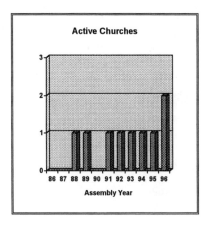

In 1996 there were 2 active Churches of the Nazarene that reported Laotian as the primary cultural group.

Laotian congregations reported a full membership of 303; average A.M. attendance of 492; and a Sunday School average of 367.

This is a net growth of 2 churches since 1986 and an increase of 303 members over the same time period.

Prepared by the Church Growth Research Center from statistics reported annually to the general secretary, January 1997.

NAZARENE GROWTH AMONG
NATIVE AMERICANS
in the United States, 1986-96

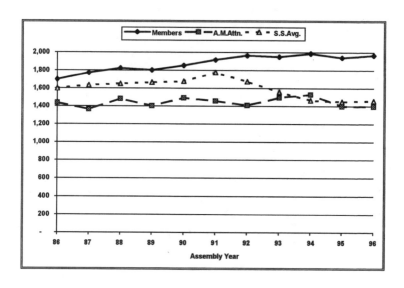

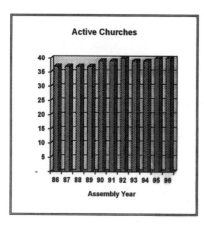

In 1996 there were 40 active Churches of the Nazarene that reported Native American as the primary cultural group.

These churches reported a combined membership of 1,971; a total A.M. attendance of 1,397; and a Sunday School average of 1,459.

This is a net growth of 3 churches since 1986 and an increase of 15.9 percent in membership over the same time period.

Prepared by the Church Growth Research Center from statistics reported annually to the general secretary, January 1997.

NAZARENE GROWTH AMONG PORTUGUESE
in the United States
1986-96

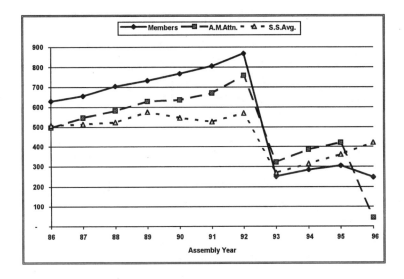

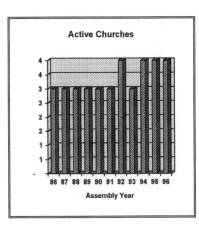

In 1996 there were 4 active Churches of the Nazarene that reported Portuguese as the primary cultural group.

These churches reported a combined membership of 247; a total A.M. attendance of 544; and a Sunday School average of 422.

This is a net growth of 1 church since 1986. One large church has since been classified as multicultural rather than Portuguese.

Prepared by the Church Growth Research Center from statistics reported annually to the general secretary, January 1997.

NAZARENE GROWTH AMONG SAMOANS
in the United States
1986-96

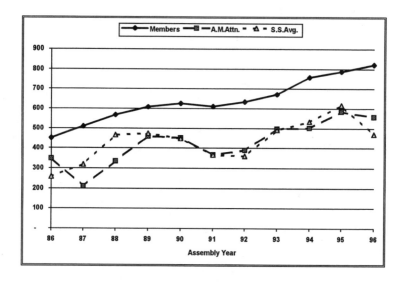

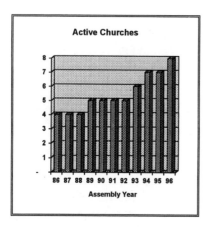

In 1996 there were 8 active Churches of the Nazarene that reported Samoan as the primary cultural group.

Samoan congregations reported a combined membership of 823; a total A.M. attendance of 558; and a Sunday School average of 471.

This is a net growth of 4 churches since 1986 and an increase of 82 percent in membership over the same time period.

Prepared by the Church Growth Research Center from statistics reported annually to the general secretary, January 1997.

NAZARENE GROWTH AMONG SOUTH ASIANS
in the United States
1986-96

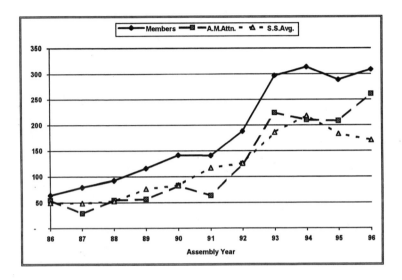

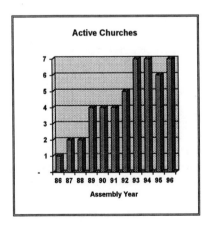

In 1996 there were 7 active Churches of the Nazarene that reported South Asian as the primary cultural group.

These churches reported a combined membership of 309; a total A.M. attendance of 261; and a Sunday School average of 171.

This is a net growth of 6 churches since 1986 and an increase of 375 percent in membership over the same time period.

Prepared by the Church Growth Research Center from statistics reported annually to the general secreatry, January 1997.

NAZARENE GROWTH AMONG VIETNAMESE
in the United States
1986-96

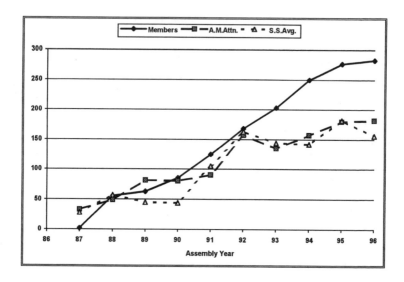

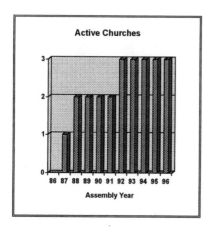

In 1996 there were 3 active Churches of the Nazarene that reported Vietnamese as the primary cultural group.

These churches reported a combined membership of 283; a total A.M. attendance of 182; and a Sunday School average of 156.

This is a net growth of 3 churches since 1986 and an increase of 283 members over the same time period.

Prepared by the Church Growth Research Center from statistics reported annually to the general secretary, January 1997.

Appendix 2

CREDENTIALED MINISTERS BY GENDER AND ROLE IN THE CHURCH OF THE NAZARNE

Year	Male Pastors	Female Pastors	% Female Pastors	Male Evangelists	Female Evangelists	% Female Evangelists	Total Males	Total Females	% Total Females
1908	140	13	8.5%	47	36	43.4%	561	121	17.7%
1915	373	33	8.1%	63	26	29.2%	1,168	197	14.4%
1920	607	83	12.0%	251	91	26.6%	1,799	435	19.5%
1925	843	117	12.2%	188	68	26.6%	2,073	527	20.3%
1930	1,087	136	11.1%	207	65	23.9%	2,469	646	20.7%
1935	1,498	176	10.5%	317	94	22.9%	3,022	767	20.2%
1940	1,893	160	7.8%	297	108	26.7%	3,633	848	18.9%
1945	2,301	150	6.1%	378	112	22.9%	4,382	878	16.7%
1950	2,828	148	5.0%	436	120	21.6%	5,371	898	14.3%
1955	3,517	234	6.2%	499	117	19.0%	6,214	875	12.3%
1960	3,772	189	4.8%	476	101	17.5%	6,501	804	11.0%
1965	3,974	148	3.6%	476	63	11.7%	7,182	724	9.2%
1970	4,046	110	2.6%	491	57	10.4%	8,077	660	7.6%
1975	4,096	82	2.0%	478	45	8.6%	9,170	605	6.2%
1980	4,150	72	1.7%	432	37	7.9%	9,618	591	5.8%
1985	4,497	52	1.1%	280	19	6.4%	9,583	508	5.0%
1990	4,584	65	1.4%	283	20	6.6%	10,371	663	6.0%
1995	4,439	76	1.7%	285	23	7.5%	10,884	783	6.7%

TOTAL CREDENTIALED MINISTERS IN THE CHURCH OF THE NAZARENE BY GENDER

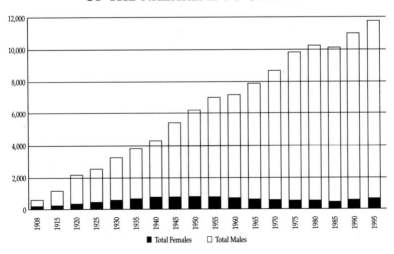

■ Total Females   □ Total Males

Appendix 3

Statement on Inclusive Language*

Grouping people by race or ethnicity is a social and political phenomenon, and, as such, these categories are not fixed. As society changes, so do the labeling conventions that define groups. In fact, many people confuse the terms "racial" and "ethnic." They are not synonymous. While a race or an ethnic group may constitute a minority in certain contexts, "minority" is less preferable as a term than designating the specific group or groups in question. The term "minority" is still used in government policies on affirmative action and equal opportunity to refer to underrepresented groups.

To reflect individuality and diversity, it is best to choose language that accords with an audience's expectations and self-image. While it is certainly preferable to designate a specific group, such as Asian Americans, American Indians, and so on, rather than using the term "minorities," these general terms also tend to overlook the rich diversity of national origin within these groups.

Recommendations:

- Refer to race, religion, or national ethnic origin only if germane to your point.
- Respect the wishes of the group to or for whom you are writing.

  Even within broadly drawn groups, individual members may not agree about which term they feel

*Adapted from *Guidelines for Using Inclusive Language and Illustrations in University Publications* (1991). By permission of the Office of University Publications, University of Maryland, College Park.

best defines them. In the United States, the terms "Black," "Black American," "Afro-American," and "African-American" coexist and are equally current. "Minority" is not a synonym for "Black."

Since the 1970s, the diversity among Asian Americans has grown from mostly Chinese and Japanese Americans to Korean, Vietnamese, Laotian, Cambodian, and Philippine Americans, people from different ethnic and cultural groups. The term "Oriental" for Asian American is inappropriate.

The terms "American Indian" and "Native American" are both in current use. Many individuals prefer to have their tribe designated when being introduced or written about.

The term "Hispanic" is in common usage on the East Coast to refer to Mexican Americans, Central Americans, Latin Americans, and Puerto Ricans. In the West, Latino/Latina is generally preferred. Chicano/Chicana refers specifically to Mexican Americans and is used especially by people who are politically active.

- Avoid descriptive words or labels that reinforce racial and ethnic stereotypes.

Not: Black slaves

But: enslaved Blacks

Not: We hire qualified women and minorities.

But: Women and minorities are encouraged to apply.

Rather than use the phrases "culturally disadvantaged" or "culturally deprived," describe the specific difference in background directly in relation to the areas of achievement under discussion. Do not associate learning patterns and abilities with specific racial or ethnic groups, but rather with social or physical conditions.

List of Commonly Encountered Terms*

alien, resident alien—Acceptable when it refers to legal status of non-United States citizens. Use when quoting official language, policy, or procedures. Note that it is not polite to call an international student or scholar an alien. (See international, foreign.)

American Indian—Often acceptable. However, the general term should be avoided if a specific tribe or nation is being referred to. Do not use such terms as "Mohawk Indian," which is redundant. (See also Native American.)

Anglo or Anglo-American—Not recommended. Use "English-speaking" or "white," depending on what is meant.

Asian—Acceptable, but be specific if possible (e.g., Chinese, Japanese). (See Oriental.)

Black—Enjoys wide acceptance, though "African-American" is increasingly preferred. McGraw-Hill and the Associated Press do not capitalize "white," considering it a generic or descriptive term and do not recommend capitalizing "black." Be consistent. Capitalize both or neither. [Note: The style of Beacon Hill Press of Kansas City, followed throughout this entire book, is to capitalize "Black" when used as either a noun or an adjective referring to this people group. "White" is capitalized as a noun but not as an adjective.]

Chicano, Chicana—Often used for Mexican Americans born in the United States.

Eskimo—The term "Inuit" is preferred by Arctic and Canadian peoples.

---

*Excerpted and adapted from *Guidelines for Bias-Free Publishing* (New York: McGraw-Hill Book Company, 1983) 27-31.

ethnic, ethnics—Colloquialism. Refers to "new immigrant" nationalities from Southern and Eastern Europe.

Foreign—"Foreign" is appropriate to use in describing places of origin or in making a distinction between categories or persons, as in making the distinction between United States and foreign students. International students and scholars realize that they are foreigners and are not normally offended by the term; however, use the word "international" whenever possible. (See alien, international.)

Hebrew—A language. Not acceptable to refer to a person or a religion, except in references to ancient Israel.

Hispanic, Hispanic American—See Latin American.

Indian—Refers to people from India. Not to be confused with "American Indian" or "Native American."

Inuk, Inuit—Preferred over "Eskimo" by Arctic and Canadian peoples.

international—In discussing people of national origin other than United States citizens, "international" is the preferred word. Students and scholars from abroad are normally referred to as international students, scholars. (See alien, foreign.)

Israeli—Citizen of Israel; not all Israelis are Jews.

Jew—People whose religion or religious background is Jewish.

Latin American—There is wide confusion over what term to use when referring to Spanish- and Portuguese-speaking people in the Western Hemisphere. "Hispanic" is often used instead of "Latin American" when referring to residents of the United States who speak Spanish or are one or two generations removed from

THE CHANGING FACE OF THE CHURCH

Spanish-speaking people from one of the Central American, South American, or Caribbean countries. However, some groups object to the term "Hispanic" on the grounds that it emphasizes a shared European cultural heritage rather than a shared New World cultural heritage.

Certainly not all Spanish-speaking people from Mexico, Central America, South America, or Caribbean countries are of Spanish descent. When possible, be specific. Some resent "Latin American," saying it is insensitive to national differences; some find it inaccurate, since not all people referred to as "Latin American" speak Latin-based languages. Further, it usually does not include French speakers.

Again, when possible, be specific. "Mexican," "Central American," or "South American" can also be used. "Ibero-American" is acceptable, but clumsy; use "Brazilian" instead of "Luso-American."

Latino/Latina—Preferred by some groups to "Hispanic."

Mexican American—Acceptable.

multicultural, multiculturalism—As an adjective, "multicultural" is synonymous with cultural pluralism, describing a variety of cultures or subcultures (including English-speaking Whites) within the United States. Do not use "multiculturals" (not a word as a noun) to refer to minority groups. "Multiculturalism" sometimes refers to the idea that no culture is better than another and at other times is interpreted to represent "cultural particularism" or "ethnocentrism," representing cultural superiority (e.g., Eurocentrism or Afrocentrism).

Muslim—Used to refer to persons whose religion is Islam. Note: the term "Muslim" is not interchangeable with "Arab."

Native American—Preferred by some groups to "American Indian." Note that when it is used with a lower-case "n" it can refer to people born in the United States (sometimes called "native-born Americans").

native peoples—Acceptable.

Negro—Acceptable when quoting from a historical document in the appropriate historical context.

Oriental—Not acceptable. Use "Asian" or be specific.

Spanish-speaking people—See Latin American.

we/our (when referring to the United States)—Not recommended.

Notes

Introduction

1. From its International Headquarters in Kansas City, the Church of the Nazarene provides ministries to the United States and Canada through the Church Growth Division and to the rest of the world through the World Mission Division. Canada is referred to often in the book because of the close working relationship of the Canadian districts and the United States districts within the Church Growth Division. Some of the demographic changes in the United States and the United States church apply in Canada. However, the particular focus of this book is the effect of demographic changes unique to the United States upon the American church.

2. The ecumenical religious publication *Christian Century* began publication during the early years of the new century, reflecting the optimism of the Progressive Era in politics and religion that this century would indeed see the values of Christianity reflected in human progress.

3. Jerry L. Appleby, *Missions Have Come Home to America: The Church's Cross-cultural Ministry to Ethnics* (Kansas City: Beacon Hill Press of Kansas City, 1986).

Chapter 1

1. Committee members in addition to John Knight and Bill Sullivan included: John C. Bowling, president, Olivet Nazarene University; Roger Bowman, superintendent, Los Angeles District; H. Melvin McCullough, pastor, Bethany, Oklahoma, First Church; Jesse C. Middendorf, pastor, Kansas City First Church; Dallas D. Mucci, superintendent, Metro New York District; Jerry Porter, superintendent, Washington District; Richard Spindle, president, MidAmerica Nazarene College; Jack Stone, general secretary, Church of the Nazarene; Gordon Wetmore, president, Nazarene Theological Seminary; Lee Woolery, superinten-

dent, Northwest Indiana District; and John W. Work, president, John W. Work Associates.

2. Available upon request from the Multicultural Ministries office: telephone 800-306-9950.

Chapter 2

1. Sam Roberts, *Who We Are* (New York: Time Books/Random House, 1994), 3-4.

2. The seven denominations are: The Assemblies of God, Catholics, Churches of Christ, Episcopalians, the Presbyterian Church U.S.A., Southern Baptists, and United Methodists.

Chapter 3

1. The reported 10 percent minority membership does not include minority members in predominately white English-speaking churches. If those estimates were included, the minority presence would likely approach 12 to 15 percent.

2. In-Gyeong Kim Lundell, *Bridging the Gaps: Contextualization Among Korean Nazarene Churches in America* (New York: Peter Lang, 1985), 95.

3. Ibid., 91.

4. Ibid., 21.

5. Ibid.

6. Raymond W. Hurn, comp., *Black Evangelism—Which Way from Here?* (Kansas City: Nazarene Publishing House, 1974), 7.

7. Ibid., 16.

Chapter 4

1. See chapter 2.

2. James A. Joseph, *Remaking America: How the Benevolent Traditions of Many Cultures Are Transforming Our National Life* (San Francisco: Jossey-Bass Publishers, 1995), 13.

3. Ibid., 216.

4. See chapter 2.

5. Contact the Multicultural Ministries office for a handbook on multicongregational ministries. Telephone 800-306-9950.

6. Donald McGavran, *Understanding Church Growth* (Grand Rapids: Wm. B. Eerdmans, 1990), 98.

7. C. Peter Wagner, *Our Kind of People: The Ethical Dimensions of Church Growth in America* (Atlanta: John Knox Press, 1979), 1.

8. Bill Sullivan, "There Is Only One Church Growth Principle," *Grow*, Winter 1994-95, inside front cover.

9. Dallas D. Mucci, "Metro New York District Leads U.S.A. Districts in Growth: Interview with District Superintendent Dallas D. Mucci," *Grow*, Winter 1993-94, 1-4.

Chapter 5

1. John W. Work, *What Every CEO Already Knows About Managing Diversity* (Highland City, Fla.: Rainbow Books, Inc., 1993).

2. John Work, "Leading a Diverse Work Force," in *The Leader of the Future*, ed. Frances Hesselbein, Marshall Goldsmith, and Richard Beckhard (New York: Peter Drucker Foundation, 1996), 78-79.

3. See chapter 2.

4. *Manual of the Church of the Nazarene, 1993-97* (Kansas City: Nazarene Publishing House, 1993), 138.

5. See chapter 2.

6. See Appendix 2 for chart on percentage of women in ministry.

7. *Manual, 1993-97*, 324, par. 904.6.

8. Contact the Multicultural Ministries office for a copy of the Handbook on Multicongregational Ministries. Telephone 800-306-9950.